The Beauty of the In-Between

FINDING GOD IN THE SILENCE, THE STRUGGLE, AND THE PLACES IN-BETWEEN

Matthew Nelson

Copyright © 2019 by Matthew Nelson.

All rights reserved. No part of this publication may be reproduced, distributed or transmitted in any form or by any means, including photocopying, recording, or other electronic or mechanical methods, without the prior written permission of the publisher, except in the case of brief quotations embodied in critical reviews and certain other noncommercial uses permitted by copyright law. For permission requests, write to the publisher, addressed "Attention: Permissions Coordinator," at the address below.

City Church Attn: Matthew Nelson
PO Box 14500
Tulsa, OK 74159
info@citychurchtulsa.com
www.mattnelsononline.com

Book Layout ©2017 BookDesignTemplates.com

Cover Design: Nick Livingston
https://nixn.co

Ordering Information:
Quantity sales. Special discounts are available on quantity purchases by corporations, associations, and others. For details, contact us at the email or address above.

The Beauty of the In-Between/ Matthew Nelson. —1st ed.
ISBN 978-1-7337667-0-8

Contents

PART I: THE PASTURE

The Places In-Between 13

The Land of Obscurity 27

Detours in Disguise 42

The Art of Being 54

PART II: THE CAVE

Emptied 64

Theology for the Middle 77

Scars 89

Clarity Addicts 101

Through the Wall 111

PART III: THE PALACE

The Secret 128

Success 142

Valleys and Pitfalls 149

Overflow 158

Legacy 169

To my wife, Lindsay: You are the single greatest joy of my life and my best friend and I'm so incredibly grateful for you.

To my children, Jaxon, Selah, Sophie, and Jude: My prayer for you is that you experience the radical and unrelenting love of your heavenly Father; a love that I can't begin to match.

To my parents, Gary and Diana: You have been a source of love and encouragement in every season of my life and the single greatest reflection of the Father's love. Thank you!

To my pastors and mentors, Rodney and Jason: You took the time to invest in a young man and let me into your home, your life, and your ministry. Thank you!

To my church, City Church: The last ten years has been the greatest journey of my life and I believe it's only just begun. Let's plant more churches, make more disciples, and see our city and the world transformed by the gospel of Jesus Christ.

Every time we finally reach the future, it vanishes into the present. This perplexing tendency of the future to keep eluding us does not, of course, teach us to be more present, but rather to accelerate faster.

— WAYNE MULLER

INTRODUCTION

"Hey, babe! Let's just go for a drive." Sometimes my wife enjoys just getting in the car and driving aimlessly. No destination in mind, just driving. After years of marriage, I've learned how to do this, but it took some time getting used to it. I don't just drive to drive; I drive to arrive at a destination. In fact, whenever I get in my car to go anywhere, my mind is already navigating the streets of my city and taking into account the time of day, current road construction, and possible shortcuts. Is there a way I can possibly avoid traffic and get there two minutes earlier? It's like a game I'm playing against myself. That's why when my wife says, "Hey, babe! Let's just go for a drive," my mind has no context for such an activity. How do I drive unless I have a destination? Who does that? My wife does that, apparently.

For years, I've heard people use cliché phrases like, "Life is about the journey, not the destination," or, "Just enjoy the ride." Even though I used to agree with the sentiment, I quickly found myself on the hamster wheel spinning tirelessly to achieve what was next.

Over the years, I've learned that life is not some destination where we arrive or some achievement we unlock; life *is* the process—the slow, unpredictable, joyous, painful, mysterious process of living. And although we may claim to embrace this idea, most of us are rather addicted to reaching the destination. We're addicted to the knowing, the arriving, the glitz and glamour of finally achieving what we set out to accomplish. But as you probably found out by now, that's just not how life works. If only it were a straight line, a linear trajectory where our lives took a gradual and steady course for the better. But, of course, it is not. Life is not a steady climb from one success to the next. Most of life actually takes place in-between.

> *Life is anything but neat, clean, or predictable, and neither is God's process. God's process is full of ups and downs, zigzags, uncertainties, struggles, seasons of doubt, and times where we feel as though God has completely forgotten us. It may not fit our plan, but it doesn't mean it's not God's process. In fact, it's highly possible that God is not trying to get us from point A to point B by the quickest route possible. Maybe there are more important things at stake than our arrival. Maybe he's intentionally taking us the long way because that's the only remedy for a truly transformed soul. Maybe, just maybe, God is big enough and sovereign enough that his process doesn't have to be direct or look anything like we think it should.*

If we are really going to embrace God's process for our lives, it means embracing the season we're in, the struggle we're going through, and the reality of where we're currently living. It means we have faith that God is in control of the situations that seem completely outside our five-year plan. It means submitting to a process that doesn't always fit within the neat, clean parameters of our rational thinking or finite understanding. It's finding God in the waiting, in the in-between.

You see, after years of studying the scriptures I began to see a pattern emerge throughout the story of God. Those who were "called," or set apart for a specific purpose by God, also experienced seasons of preparation; an intense time of testing when faith was no longer an allusive concept to be believed but an action that required everything they could muster. It's been said, "God deeply wounds those he uses." His servants must experience true brokenness before they are prepared to face the challenges of being used for his purposes. If you don't believe me, then I encourage you to open your Bible to almost anywhere. Whether it's God telling Abraham to sacrifice his son Isaac in Genesis 22, or Jacob serving Laban for fourteen years before receiving Rachel as his bride in Genesis 29. There is Joseph in Genesis 39, who received a dream from God but found himself unjustly accused of rape and put in prison. Or Moses in Exodus 2, who runs into the desert after killing an Egyptian and spends forty years as a shepherd to his father-in-law Jethro. God is continually enrolling certain men and women in a process that he will use to significantly impact the kingdom of God.

Take a look at every backstory. Look at the struggle, the pain, the years of waiting that so many of God's "called" had to endure. Is that wasted time? Is that proof that God simply does not want to promote his children? Or is God up to something greater? God wants to take us through a process, and more than likely it will entail something that none of us will necessarily want to sign up for: BROKENNESS and SURRENDER.

The only problem with God's process is that most people will be perfectly content with doing it their own way. They will choose to arrive at the destination more quickly and with far fewer detours. But could it be they're missing out on what it's really all about? Could it be that by taking a shortcut through God's process we're actually missing the very thing we're really searching for? Is it possible we can arrive at our so-called destination and simultaneously miss it?

This book is about the places you will inevitably walk through if you choose to embrace God's process for your life. And as badly as we may want progress at any cost, this book isn't about the three quickest ways to navigate God's process or the ten necessary steps to unlocking God's perfect will for your life. It isn't about developing a surefire plan to negotiate what's next, or five laws to shorten your waiting period. It's not about how to alleviate all the pain of life or to arrive at your destination more quickly. It's about embracing each and every place on the journey. It's about reflecting on the scars, pushing forward in the pain, and learning that clarity isn't always what it's cracked up to be. It's about learning that the places in-between are not to be despised, but are often the very places where God is discovered in a new and profound way. They are full of mystery, beauty, and wonder, if only we will take the time to stop and take notice.

During my fourteen years of full-time ministry, I have coached and counseled hundreds of people through their "in-between" seasons of life, and I have found myself having the same conversations over and over again. As a church planter and entrepreneur, I've been forced to navigate the ups and downs, the highs and lows of both success and failure, and somewhere along the way I realized that most of us are chasing something. The reason I wrote this book is that somewhere along my journey I stopped chasing and realized that what I was so desperately pursuing was not somewhere right around the next corner—but was right here and right now. I want that for you! I want you to find the beauty that is found in embracing the place you're in and not obsessing over the not-yet.

The journey we are about to embark on follows the life of King David and David's journey was anything but linear. In fact, there were numerous unplanned stops he made along the way that significantly shaped his life. We'll visit the pasture, the cave, and the palace along with David. The pasture represents the place of obscurity that we often despise because it lacks the sexiness and appeal of the spotlight. And yet, I'm still learning how absolutely essential this pasture season is to my life and character. Next, the cave represents the moments when life doesn't go according to plan. The cave is the confusion, the brokenness, or the difficulties that are an inevitable part of life's journey. I've learned, however, that the cave can bring us into a new and profound place in our relationship with God that otherwise we would have never found. And, last, the palace represents the place where we are living our lives out of the overflow of a relationship with Christ.

Maybe in the following chapters you will find yourself situated somewhere in the story of King David. You might not visit an actual pasture, cave, or palace, but I can guarantee you will face a place of identity, surrender, and purpose on your journey of faith. You will experience the uncertainty, the pain, the doubts, the fears, the tests, and the difficult lesson of learning to embrace God's process for your life.

If you're looking for a quick motivational tool on how to achieve success, principles for improving your career, or how to get the perfect job, you've come to the wrong place and you're about to be wildly disappointed. Take my advice and turn back now. If you're willing to embrace God's process, find him in the waiting, and befriend the lifelong journey of surrender and brokenness, then welcome to God's school of discipleship: the only internship that guarantees and completely redefines success.

PART I: THE PASTURE

"Jesse had seven of his sons pass before Samuel, but Samuel said to him, 'The Lord has not chosen these.' So, he asked Jesse, 'Are these all the sons you have?' 'There is still the youngest,' Jesse answered. 'He is tending the sheep.' Samuel said, 'Send for him; we will not sit down until he arrives.'" (1 Samuel 16:10-11)

> *The pasture is a place for forgotten people. The place where you are overlooked, undervalued, or maybe even unknown. It's also the breeding ground for greatness. The pasture is not just a place along the journey; it's a necessity. Without it, we inevitably become a Saul: a born leader with natural gifts who, in his moment of distress and testing, chose to preserve his image rather than obey the commands of God. The pasture is not a place we graduate from or a season of life we simply pass through on the way to our desired destination. The pasture ultimately determines who we will become. Our identity is forged in the pasture.*

The pasture is a place of obscurity. It tests our motives, delves into the recesses of our hearts, and quietly reveals the foundations upon which we are establishing our identity. If you're looking for the spotlight, applause, or the next accolade, then the pasture isn't for you. If you've never learned the art of "being," then you will inevitably zoom right through the pasture en route to your destination, leaving it in your rearview mirror at seventy-five miles per hour.

In 1 Samuel, the people of Israel finally got their wish, a king named Saul to rule over them in power. They wanted a person, in the flesh, who could lead them into battle, settle their disputes, make their decisions, and become the face of their nation. But Israel didn't account for the pride that consumes the hearts of leaders, especially those who aren't broken.

Little did they know that in a pasture just outside Bethlehem, one of the greatest leaders the world would ever see, a man after the very heart of God, was learning to embrace the obscurity of the pasture. Little did anyone know that greatness could be birthed in the unknown; that true power could take root in the humblest of places.

I want you to really think about the life and calling of King David. Here he was, a young boy tending the sheep out in the pasture, and he gets called up to the house because there is a visitor. When he enters the house, he recognizes an aged man as the prophet Samuel. He must have wondered why the prophet would be at his house of all places. Next thing he knows, Samuel is standing next to him, staring David in the face and grabbing him by the arm as oil begins running down his face. He's been anointed the next king over all of Israel. "But doesn't Israel already have a king?" David asks. "What about Saul? And how could it be someone as young and unremarkable as me?"

From here the story jumps around until we see the people of Israel standing in the Valley of Elah being taunted by Goliath, the Philistine warrior. The text specifically tells us in 1 Samuel 17:14-15: "David was the youngest. The three oldest (brothers) followed Saul, but David went back and forth from Saul to tend his father's sheep at Bethlehem."

Here is David, the next king over all of Israel, who still has a day job as a shepherd, which is possibly the most pedestrian job imaginable. This is not necessarily the internship most would choose for a future king, and yet it might have been the ideal setting to produce "a man after the heart of God." The pasture was the ultimate place of obscurity. There was nobody to impress; it was just David and the sheep. It was a place where he was alone with his thoughts and had to wrestle with his faith and the implications of being anointed the next king over Israel. It's possible these moments of solitude, this time on the backside of the pasture, came to define the life of David. Remove all our external motivators and the ability to impress, compare, or receive praise, and we find who we really are.

Could it be that the place we despise the most is the very place that will prove to be the most essential? Could it be that the moments of solitude and obscurity force us to look a little deeper into our souls than we are comfortable with?

The pasture confronts us with the reality of our situation and the purity of our motives. You could even say the pasture, these moments of complete obscurity, are the truest indicator of the heart of an individual. Will we embrace the obscurity, will we trust in God's process, or will we despise it? The pasture can become either a graveyard or a boot camp for the dreams God has placed in our hearts. The question is not, "Will I enter the pasture?", but, "What will I do when I find myself there?"

Consider the implications the pasture had on the life of David. It was the life of a shepherd that taught David responsibility and how to manage a small business operation. The pasture became the place where songs, hymns, and prayers were inspired and written. It was the place where the harp went from a casual pastime to something far greater. It was the place where a slingshot went from a toy to a weapon and a young man discovered how to be a warrior, fighting off a lion and a bear. Maybe most of all, it was in the pasture where David discovered his identity, something that would sustain him through every mountaintop and valley he would come to experience.

Although David could have complained, he saw it as an opportunity to train. He could have been discouraged, but instead he chose to worship. People who have embraced the land of obscurity are not so addicted to the future that they fail to see what God is up to in the middle of the mundane.

The pasture, defined by obscurity and solitude, is essential to gaining our IDENTITY. And without knowing who we are and who God is, we will never be fully surrendered; we will never fully embrace God's process. So let's walk through the pasture together. It may not be as glorious as we desire, but it might be the very thing we need the most.

CHAPTER 1

The Places In-Between

The Backside of the Pasture

After I graduated high school, I was in a difficult place and uncertain about what to do with my future. Five days after graduation, my youth pastor, who had resigned to help plant a church six-months earlier, called me and asked me about my summer plans. My summer and my foreseeable future were wide open at the moment, which is a nice way to say I was lost in life. He told me they had just planted a church in January of 2002, and I could come and be an intern. They currently had about thirty to forty people attending the church, and he would move his two kids into a room together and give me the spare bedroom. As long as I was okay with Toy Story bedsheets and a job description that included everything imaginable, I could join them. I'm honestly not sure if it was my desire to be in ministry, a desire to get out of my parents' home, or just the impending uncertainty of my future, but I eagerly accepted. Little did I know how that summer would shape my future.

As an intern that summer I was the graphic designer, setup/teardown crew, youth pastor, small group leader, and anything else you could possibly imagine. We were now fifty to sixty people meeting in a middle school "cafetorium" (that's when you combine an auditorium and cafeteria), and the best books on church planting hadn't been written yet.

One Sunday morning that summer, my pastor preached about David, the shepherd boy, in the middle school cafetorium. For whatever reason, growing up I was always drawn to the story of David. It wasn't just about Goliath for me; it was that David seemed to be part songwriter, part gladiator, part pastor, part warrior, all wrapped up into one person who was labeled "a man after the heart of God." The complexity of David's life still baffles me. That Sunday the message was about learning to embrace the pasture, the backside of the wilderness where David learned to fall in love with God. Something began in my heart that day, and I'm still wrestling with the implications to this day. It was this deep-seeded understanding that before I needed to perform, achieve, or arrive at some destination, I had to first learn the difficult journey of being with him—of embracing the now and not obsessing over the not-yet or the what-could-be. If not, I would spend my whole life chasing.

At the end of that summer, I was sitting in the registrar's office on the campus of the University of Central Oklahoma waiting to get my schedule for the upcoming fall semester. It was two weeks before school started; there were thirty other people in the waiting area, and my name was twelfth on the waiting list. I was going to take classes that fall while simultaneously leading the youth ministry for the small church plant I had recently been a part of. Becoming a youth pastor was all I had wanted to do ever since giving my heart to Christ as a fourteen-year-old student.

As I sat there, I never heard an audible voice, I never opened my Bible to the perfect verse, and nobody came by to give me a specific word. I just felt deep down in my soul that something about what I was doing wasn't right. I was sacrificing what was "best" for what was "good" and what was "now." I sat in a chair for the next forty-five minutes watching students interact and one-by-one go into the office and come back out. It seemed like any old Tuesday afternoon for most, but I was wrestling with something that would greatly affect my future for years to come.

I heard my name called, and I headed to the office door. I can still remember the internal struggle that was ensuing inside me even as I walked the fifteen feet from my chair to the office. I walked in, looked at the registrar frantically maneuvering the papers on her desk, and I just stood motionless in the doorway. She motioned for me to come and have a seat, and I remember replying in a sheepish, wavering voice: "Thank you, but I won't be attending this university this fall. I'm sorry I wasted your time." She was about to make a reply, but I didn't wait to hear what it was. I was out the door and walking through the hallway of the student center before I could make sense of what just happened.

A few weeks earlier I had applied to another university about an hour and a half away where I could pursue a degree in ministry and biblical studies. It was honestly more of a backup plan. The first university seemed like a sure bet and a wide-open door to my future dreams. It was right in front of me, and the job was already on the table. The second university was a gamble. It was farther away but could potentially prepare me for my future in a way the first university could not. It can be difficult to take a risk when a seemingly surefire opportunity is right there. One week before classes started, I loaded up my Chevy pickup and drove 100 miles down the turnpike to the second university where I knew one person—not even someone I liked.

I was just a few weeks into my college journey, and things weren't going as planned. My roommate was twenty-five years old and had spent most of his life in China as a missionary kid. He had an obsession with martial arts: not the cool kind where you can beat people up, but this bizarre practice where he would have people punch him in the throat or kick him between the legs as hard as they could, and he would block out the pain. Okay, honestly that part was a lot of fun, but it was still weird. He was also obsessed with Quentin Tarantino films, especially *Pulp Fiction*, which he would watch multiple times each week. Other than that, he would play *Grand Theft Auto* or *Halo* almost every hour of the day. Between him and my 7:50 a.m. biology class, I began thinking, "There is no way I passed up my dream of being a youth pastor for this." I had abandoned the very thing I had desired the most, a ministry position, for a place I didn't want to be.

> *This was my first taste of the pasture, but it wouldn't be my last. The pasture would become the defining place in my life. I would have to learn the difficult and messy process of embracing God's timing and learning to love where he had me right now, not where I wanted to be or some preferred destination that didn't yet exist. I couldn't embrace the right now if I was obsessed with the future.*

I believe the lesson of embracing God's process is a lifelong journey. Over the past seventeen years it has become my life message. It has helped me navigate through mountaintops, valleys, uncertainties, doubts, transitions, and huge leaps of faith. It has helped me remain centered; focused on what really matters no matter what may be happening externally. It has helped me make my "happy place" where God has me and not some undetermined place or time in the future.

I had always assumed that this was one life lesson among many that would follow, something God wanted to teach me on my spiritual journey as I continued to climb the ladder of "success" and pursue the "calling" that was on my life. It was a necessary stop on the journey but something that I could graduate from if I would simply learn the lesson, apply it to my life, and continue moving forward.

Yet, here I am. It's been seventeen years from that moment, and I've still not graduated from this life lesson. Life has not always been a straightforward journey and now my view of the "backside of the pasture" is less about getting through and more about how to truly embrace it. It's become less about graduating from this reality and more about learning to live in it.

This lesson has deeply impacted my life, but I haven't arrived or found the secret. I continue to find myself wandering, and every next step, every achievement, every victory, and every failure continues to pervade my soul with the deep, longing question: "Who am I, and why am I here?" I've become shamelessly aware of the idols that continue to infiltrate my soul and how I've become an expert at well-intentioned, overtly spiritual idolatry. We think we're just one big break, one next step, one promotion, one _____ from the place where we'll find true contentment. And yet, it remains elusive: right around the corner or just a few steps away or just slightly beyond where we are in this very moment.

But every now and then we STOP. Stop just long enough to realize that our life is consumed by constantly chasing that thing, that something deep within us we falsely believe will somehow unlock our deepest longing. In fact, many of us spend our whole lives chasing something that is continually slipping through our fingers.

If I could go back seventeen years from this moment, look myself in the eye, and tell that person what I would be doing today, I can guarantee you a smile would come across the face of younger me. I would rejoice in the notion that I could make my life's work about pastoring people, making disciples, training church planters, and fighting on behalf of the children in our city in the foster care system who don't have a forever family. But even today there is an unquenched longing in my soul, a pervasive desire to try to find what's next.

In the following pages, I invite you into this journey with me; but let me be very frank about what you're going to read. Many people teach out of their expertise, out of their ability to overcome, or out of their desire to communicate some sort of revelatory truth. I have not perfected the journey of the in-between, but I've spent the last several years of my life leaning into the tension. The reason this message is so powerful to me is because it puts its finger on my greatest insecurity. It unmasks my deepest longings and beckons me to continually reevaluate the motives, direction, and purpose of each of my pursuits.

Now that we have that straightened out, let's go!

Love the Process

I've learned that in hindsight everything seems better than it really is. I remember the good ol' days, but when I'm actually living in the good ol' days, I can't wait for what is next. We simply have a tendency to remember things as bigger or better than they really are. Psychologists have termed this concept as memory bias, the understanding that our fond memories as a child are usually super-sized compared to the reality of those experiences.

Growing up, I loved my grandparents' place out in the country of southern Oklahoma where I could run wild, help them make the oil wells, and do whatever I wanted. I slept in a tent, road my motorbike, built a tree house, shot my BB gun, and played with my army men in the creek. It was absolute freedom for a young boy. After my grandmother passed away, I no longer had any reason to drive out to the property. Several years later, I drove out to their old house. I never remembered it being so small. The massive oak tree where I had built my treehouse growing up now looked rather modest. The memories had become larger-than-life. The memories had become greater than the reality.

Just like those memories, nobody ever likes "the process" when you're in it. It's only fun to talk about in hindsight as you remember those so-called wilderness, valley, and desert experiences you were able to navigate. You may remember those seasons rather fondly now, but I guarantee that in the moment those days couldn't pass fast enough.

It's the place, just like the Israelites wandering in the wilderness, where we feel stuck between our God-designed destiny and our current reality. We should be closer to our destination and instead we feel like we're walking in a giant circle or completely in the dark. The wilderness is usually defined by terms such as perseverance, character, faithfulness, and hard work. That's light-years away from the place of success, gratification, and arrival we so desperately desire.

In fact, when we feel like we're stuck in the giant, never-ending process, we might even think that we've missed it along the way. We should have gone left but we went right, and now we're being forced to endure the wilderness. Now we're in a big holding tank: the place where all forward motion has been halted and the waiting commences. If we've lived very long, then it's inevitable we will arrive at a place where our expectations and reality are on different planets. It's in these moments that our faith is challenged. We're tempted to give up hope, let go of our dreams, abandon our call, revert to doubting, and assume that if it hasn't happened, then it won't happen. Learning to embrace God's process, his bigger plan for our life, will require us to take a huge step of faith. The waiting will require us to muster everything we know to be true about who God is!

Take a minute and think about what happens in "the process." It's usually in those despised seasons of obscurity that the most inward transformation takes place. It's the place where trust is formulated, character is refined, perseverance is tested, and motives are evaluated.

When we become addicted to the destination, we usually end up despising the process. Maybe, just maybe, if we learned to fully embrace what God was trying to do in the process, we could actually shorten our season in the wilderness.

Do you think it was God's plan to have the Israelite lollygag in the desert, fight and quarrel, and slaughter several thousand of their own people? I seriously doubt it. The wilderness was all about development: preparation for the Promised Land. In fact, we could even say that the wilderness was a necessary prerequisite for the Promised Land. And, in many regards, the Israelites failed their test. They reverted back to quarreling, complaining, and idolizing every time something didn't go their way. So much so that God had to raise up a new generation in the wilderness who would be prepared for the tests of the Promised Land. If God is not enough in the wilderness, then he won't be enough in the Promised Land (but we'll get to that a little later).

While we may despise the process, it's not an optional part of life. Can you imagine what would happen if God always took us straight from deliverance to destination? I can only imagine how many people would sit around in the Promised Land singing songs of their own glory and efforts. What began as a miraculous work of God would soon become nothing more than a mighty work of our own strength. Just think of the songs, monuments, trophies, and accolades we would inevitably make unto our own glory!

Some might say that you never stop being in process, and while there is definite truth to that, there's also no denying that some seasons are way more intense than others. Maybe you're in a season that doesn't look like what you thought it would. Maybe you're in a waiting pattern or transition. Maybe you've been blindsided by life, and your dreams and future seem to be dangling over the abyss of despair. All of these require you to believe that God is at work, that he is involved in every detail of your life, and that if you submit yourself to his process, he will develop something in you. It requires faith to believe that God is good, not 99 percent good and open to the possibility of leading you into destruction, but 100 percent good and always leading you into what is best.

Let me take this one step farther. I'm not sure it's enough to only embrace God's process. I believe a key to living out an authentic walk with Christ is to cultivate a love of the process. This means we don't love the accolades or the awards or the recognition as much as we love the process: the endless journey of becoming the person God wants us to be. To find ourselves completely and fully in him.

In the Sermon on the Mount (Matthew 5-7), Jesus confronts us with our motives for kingdom living. It is no longer sufficient that we follow the rules for the wrong reasons. We can't maintain a façade of righteousness that seeks the applause of others and still consider ourselves as having a kingdom heart. This is hypocrisy. This is using God to get what we want and hoping that goodness will somehow flow from right action. It doesn't. It can't. Goodness is always rooted in God, which begins to flow from our hearts out of a genuine intimacy with our heavenly Father. We must learn to love the process, not just the rewards of the process.

Let's think of this like a professional athlete. Ask any professional athlete what they desire to accomplish, and the majority of the time you're going to hear something about being the best to play their position and/or winning a championship. Those goals become like carrots constantly dangling in front of them, giving them constant motivation for the process. While there is nothing wrong with setting goals for being the best or winning a championship, the reality is that about 95 to 99 percent of everyone who plays their sport will not accomplish either of these goals. In order for a professional athlete to find joy in their craft, they have to fall in love with the process; the grind, the struggle, the practices, the workouts, the constant tweaking and adjusting to be the very best. You don't fall in love with the idea of being the best or winning a championship; you fall in love with the process that makes those goals a reality.

In his book *The Good and Beautiful God,* James Bryan Smith talks about how we change through the process of indirection.[1] We change the things we can control in order to change the things we can't control. He tells a story about Peyton Manning winning Super Bowl XLI, which is the only Super Bowl ever played in the rain. Peyton Manning didn't play well simply because he desired to do so or because he claimed to be the best. He played well because every two weeks he would go out into an open field with his center, Jeff Saturday, and a group of wide receivers, and he would practice snapping, throwing, and catching in the mud with water-soaked footballs. That practice translated into his ability to outplay Rex Grossman of the Chicago Bears in the Super Bowl in the pouring rain. Peyton Manning fell in love with the process, which translated into him becoming one of the greatest quarterbacks to ever play the game and a Super Bowl champion.

It's the same in our lives. If we are in love with the destination but despise the process, then we will live in a constant state of discontentment and inability. It's the process that brings about the destination we all inwardly desire. It's doing the things we can do in order to influence the things we can't do. It's doing the things we can control to help direct the things we can't control.

Loving the process means loving the difficult things: the hard things that lead to the best things. Have you ever noticed how rarely you ever regret doing what is difficult? Whether it's a hard day's work, an intense workout, finishing a class, waking up early, or helping a friend in need, there is something special about submitting ourselves to what is difficult and watching the fruit of that effort turn into joy. We all know this is a hard truth to accept. It forces us to pass on the temporary pleasures of "right now" for the deeper joy that is found in commitment to what is difficult.

I've noticed how often we fail to understand this principle. We are so concerned with our happiness that we allow our decision-making to be driven through the filter, "Will this make me happy?" If we believe it will, then we will gladly exchange the long-term consequences for short-term feelings. It's now become culturally acceptable in our culture, and sadly even in the church, for a man or woman to walk away from their marriage because, "We are no longer happy." Little do we know that we are often trading the potential for deep, abiding joy for a momentary feeling that will rise and fall depending on our circumstances.

As we embrace or even fall in love with God's process, we no longer become a slave to what we feel or what is now. We live in the understanding that so many of the greatest things in life don't come easily, quickly, or by accident. In fact, the pasture, no matter how difficult it may be, only serves to enhance our ability to appreciate the process. It causes us to lean in when something else inside tells us to get out.

An Undivided Heart

I'll never forget a specific moment when I was struggling to accept the place in which God had me. I really felt like I deserved to be at the next place in my life, and God was holding me back against my will. It seemed as though my entire relationship with God revolved around my desire for God to promote me to the next place. *Why wasn't I experiencing it? What was holding me back? What did I need to do?* I thought to myself: Something must be broken in me or my faith, or I wouldn't still be here.

A wise mentor in my life recognized the misguided efforts of my attention and affectionately told me, "Matt, if God is only a stepping stone and not your source, you will inevitably give yourself the credit one day." Little did I know how true these words would become.

> *When we see God's process as wasted time on the journey to our destination and not an opportunity for a deeper, more passionate relationship with Christ, we begin using God for our own benefit. We will seek what is in his hand and not his face. We will see every situation through a clouded lens of our own effort and pursuit.*

I could learn this now in the quiet desert of solitude, or I could shortcut the process and relearn it later, which would usually cause more pain or even public humiliation.

Do you remember King Saul? The Israelites looked around at all the other peoples of the land and wondered why they didn't have a king. Why were they the only people who served a God who wasn't visible? Although it may not have been God's desire for his people, he ultimately gave them what they asked for: a king.

Saul was the epitome of a leader who looks the part. He's the good-looking guy in school who graduates as valedictorian. He's the captain of the football team who dates the head cheerleader and people just line up to follow him. You take one look at him, and he screams LEADER!

If you've read the life of Saul in 1 Samuel, then you know there are two instances that defined his kingship. Both instances required a king who was fully surrendered to the ways of God. They required a king who was more interested in obedience to Yahweh than arriving at a destination, defeating his enemies, or gaining a good reputation from the elders of Israel.

In 1 Samuel 13:8, Saul had rounded up the troops and marched to Gilgal, where they were awaiting Samuel to present the burnt offering before they entered into battle with the Philistines. This was not only a mandate from God, but a symbol that it was God going before them to provide the victory. Samuel was supposed to arrive in seven days, but he didn't. The Israelite army was anxious, King Saul was ready to attack, and the situation seemed primed for an Israelite victory. Saul grew impatient. When Samuel didn't arrive right on time, Saul took matters into his own hands and sacrificed the burnt offering and peace offering himself, which was an act specifically given to the prophet of God, not the king.

As a child, did you ever do something, and right as you were acting disobedient your parents arrived? Welcome to the life of Saul. 1 Samuel 13:10 says, "As soon as he had finished offering the burnt offering, behold, Samuel came." The smoke had not even had time to die out on the offering, and here Samuel the prophet walked up utterly confused. When Samuel confronted Saul, Saul did what most people in this situation would do: he somehow spiritualized or rationalized his disobedience. Saul, knowing it wasn't his place to make the burnt offering, framed the situation in a way where he was simply inquiring God's favor in battle, and who wouldn't want to do that? With just a little spiritual jargon, now Saul seemed to be the righteous one.

It may seem rather easy to point our finger at Saul; how difficult could it be to wait when so much seemed to be on the line? When we aren't sure if Samuel is just around the corner or is still days, weeks, or months away. What if I wait and I miss this opportunity, or what if Samuel never shows up at all?

The second instance in Saul's life is even more telling. Samuel told Saul to engage the Amalekites and completely destroy them and everything they owned for their wickedness, especially for what they had done to the people of Israel years earlier. Saul engaged the Amalekites, completely defeated them, and took King Agag as prisoner. Saul also spared the best of the sheep, oxen, fattened calves, lambs, "and all that was good, and would not utterly destroy them" (1 Samuel 15:9). Herein lies possibly the greatest danger for leaders who are unbroken and have not surrendered to God. A leader who is not broken, who has not fully embraced God's process, will ultimately sell out when pressure is applied. They will begin believing that partial obedience is the same as complete obedience. They will allow their pride and the idols occupying the throne of their hearts to ultimately win out. We know from this story and from our own lives that if Christ does not completely own our heart, we will inevitably sell out to that idol when it matters the most.

Although there is a tendency to project ourselves as better than we are, what we become in the pasture is who we will be in the palace. If we choose to claim a false identity, then in the moment of testing it will be revealed in our lives.

Patient Trust

Above all, trust in the slow work of God.

We are quite naturally impatient in everything

to reach the end without delay.

We should like to skip the intermediate stages.

We are impatient of being on the way to something

unknown, something new.

And yet it is the law of all progress

that it is made by passing through

some stages of instability—

and that it may take a very long time.

And so, I think it is with you;

your ideas mature gradually—let them grow,

let them shape themselves, without undue haste.

Don't try to force them on,

as though you could be today what time

(that is to say, grace and circumstances

acting on your own good will)

will make of you tomorrow.

Only God could say what this new spirit

gradually forming within you will be.

Give our Lord the benefit of believing

that his hand is leading you,

and accept the anxiety of feeling yourself

in suspense and incomplete.

—Pierre Teilhard de Chardin, SJ

excerpted from *Hearts on Fire*[2]

CHAPTER 2

The Land of Obscurity

The Backstory

Everybody wants to be CEO. Nobody wants to retire from the mailroom. Everybody wants to be the lead actor instead of the perennial extra. Everybody wants to be the rockstar, but some of us have to be a roadie or drive the tour bus. Ask a child, "What do you want to be when you grow up?" Rarely will you ever hear them say, "I want to be unknown, unimportant, and inconspicuous." Talk to a kid on the high school football team, and you will never hear them say, "I hope to ride the bench my entire career."

Quite the contrary, most people want to do something great, something noteworthy, something that others will look at and say, "That person is a success." Whether you have a personal drive to succeed or expectations placed on you by others, most of us would agree that we have a deep inward desire to achieve at some level. We want to be recognized. We want to be praised. We want to do something significant.

When success is the end result, most people will do whatever it takes to get there. They're constantly looking for the next job opening, internship, degree, business partnership, shortcut, etc. Whatever it takes to catapult them to that next place in life.

Success, however, is an elusive term. It's elusive in that there is no benchmark to adequately define it, and, when it is defined, it's usually done by others around us. Not only is success almost impossible to define, it's also extremely addictive. When we crave it, it can easily become the center of our entire existence. It becomes an endless, uncelebrated pursuit of something that was indefinable from the beginning, because what is subjective can never be fully attained.

Obscurity is something that is rarely celebrated in people's lives. Nobody wants to recall a period of life when we were inconspicuous. If we do recall those moments, it's only briefly and often an attempt to make us feel better about our own personal plight. Instead, we focus on the successes, the wins, and the steps towards progress.

Have you ever noticed how people don't enjoy hearing about our accomplishments as much as they do our backstory? They want to hear the story of struggle, perseverance, and failure that finally led us to the place we're at today. Why is that? Not everyone can identify with our success, but everyone can identify with our struggle. Our weakness is like Velcro that others can attach themselves to. And if we stop long enough to listen to the men and women we respect and admire the most, we will realize there is always a backstory. There is always a we-ran-out-of-money, we-were-denied-five-times, we-were-forced-to-pivot-our-strategy, we-were-betrayed-by-someone-close type of backstory. What makes the accomplishment so rewarding is directly related to the difficulty of the process.

And everyone loves a good story! You would never go to the movies simply to watch the outcome in the last ten minutes. Think about what makes a great story; it's the backstory. We wouldn't ever watch a movie that was one hour and forty-five minutes of resolution. The resolution is only enjoyable because it actually resolves a conflict.

My favorite movie of all time is *Gladiator*. Can you imagine walking into the movie just to watch Commodus's dead body lying in the gladiator arena as they are carrying Maximus's body above their heads? We would miss all the backstory: the details, the setbacks, the failures, and the difficulties that led Maximus to that very place. We wouldn't know that he used to be a great commander under Emperor Marcus Aurelius, that his family was murdered, that Commodus tried to kill him, that he made his way through the ranks of being a gladiator before making it to the Roman Coliseum, or that he was trying to restore the honor and dignity of Rome by killing Commodus. The better the backstory, the better the story will be.

I'm fearful that far too many people want the great ending without the backstory. We want the benefits without paying the price. Again, we want the rewards without embracing the process. If we can skip the period of discipline, difficult decisions, perseverance, and anonymity, then why wouldn't we simply choose to walk into success? The backstory, however, shapes who we become. It's a necessary part of the process. Difficult things produce the most lasting and fruitful results. In fact, unless we surrender the results to God and embrace the reality that we may not ever be "successful," then we will remain trapped in the cage of our expectations. Great stories do not come easily. Somewhere along the way, somebody made a series of extremely difficult decisions, sacrificed something great, and repeatedly chose to get back up after facing failure.

When we talk about the great inventor Thomas Edison, nobody opens with his first few years of futility and thousands upon thousands of failed experiments. When we speak of Steve Jobs, very few recall the early and mid 80's when Jobs not only failed but was let go by Apple. Henry Ford went broke five times before successfully starting Ford Motor Company. Walt Disney was fired from one of his first newspaper jobs because he apparently lacked imagination and had very few good ideas. For every great story of success there is usually a story of obscurity. A backstory that is marred by blunders, failed attempts, and, most of all, perseverance.

I can't help but look at the news about musicians, athletes, and actors and actresses who experience instant stardom and fame as a child or teenager, and feel heartbroken for them. They're immediately thrust into the spotlight with the world watching their every move and scrutinizing their every mistake. Many people probably envy their position, but I know I'm personally glad there wasn't a camera crew following me around when I was sixteen years old. There is a general expectation that because they are famous or have a unique ability in some area, their character should match their talent.

We are shocked when a nineteen-year-old athlete who has just been given millions of dollars is found to be struggling with drug abuse, has spent all their money in a short time, or is involved in an altercation at a nightclub. This is not saying these individuals don't work incredibly hard at their craft, but have they gone through the obscurity, isolation, or backstory that sustains us in our positions of leadership? Has their character been given time to develop?

You can fake it for a while, but inevitably your onstage performance will be indicative of your backstage life. If you don't give time and attention to the backstage of your life, then you might become a one-hit wonder. And we all know that the stage is extremely addictive. It pulls us into thinking as long as we perform like we're supposed to, then everything will be alright. It pulls us into believing that if everyone tells us we are great, then we must truly be great. Don't be fooled by the stage. It's not a true indicator of success, even though it's often the only indicator others are looking for.

The backstory may not be something you dream about or something others praise, but it's an essential part of your story.

Shelved

As a dad to four children, I have a cinema degree in anything Disney or Pixar. I've seen these movies more times than I care to admit, and I can easily sing the words to nearly every song. There is a scene from the movie *Toy Story 2*, where Andy is playing with Woody and the seam on Woody's arm rips. Instead of taking Woody to cowboy camp, Woody gets shelved next to Squeaker, the other broken toy who had been shelved. It might sound a little simplistic, but we've probably all felt that way in our life. We go unnoticed or are passed over, and we feel the pain and rejection. We get broken, wounded, or make a huge mistake, and now all our future dreams seem to die. Have you ever been shelved? Set aside? Relegated to the sidelines or the bench? It's not fun.

I can vividly remember a junior-high basketball game when I got put on the bench and realized I might be spending the rest of my basketball career in this exact spot. I had been an above-average athlete as a child, but now the other kids were getting taller, hitting puberty and growing muscles, while I just kept getting skinnier and skinnier. You know your basketball career is in decline when the major objective before each game is not getting playing time, but snagging one of the two or three pairs of jersey shorts that aren't three sizes too big. I can remember going through the entire warmup before a basketball game trying to hold up a pair of basketball shorts that were three sizes too big for my 5'6", 120-pound, seventh grade frame. It was a tough pill for me to swallow, but it was reality.

I can only imagine that David, the anointed king-to-be, felt a little bit that same way out in the pasture. Although King David achieved more in his lifetime than most could ever dream of, King David is most notably recognized for slaying the giant Goliath. It's a classic success story. An overnight rags-to-riches, *Rudy*-esque, against-all-odds kind of story.

But, you guessed it: there is a long backstory. The land of obscurity started way before David walked onto the battlefield and stood before Goliath with stone and slingshot in hand. In fact, when David told King Saul that he would go out to fight the giant Goliath, Saul immediately pointed out that David was only a boy. Saul wasn't aware of the backstory, the long, difficult journey that brought David to this place.

"But David said to Saul, 'Your servant has been keeping his father's sheep. When a lion or a bear came and carried off a sheep from the flock, I went after it, struck it and rescued the sheep from its mouth. When it turned on me, I seized it by its hair, struck it and killed it. Your servant has killed both the lion and the bear; this uncircumcised Philistine will be like one of them, because he has defied the armies of the living God. The Lord who delivered me from the paw of the lion and the paw of the bear will deliver me from the hand of this Philistine.' Saul said to David, 'Go, and the Lord be with you.'" (1 Samuel 17:34-37)

David was doing some incredible things in the land of obscurity. First of all, David spent many days and nights developing a deep, intimate relationship with God. It was a relationship that defined his life, and what I believe ultimately defined him as "a man after God's heart" (1 Samuel 13:14; Acts 13:22). It was a relationship that dictated his decisions and kept him from selling out to others or shortcutting God's divine plan for his life.

Second, David worked his tail off in the land of obscurity. Although known as a lowly shepherd boy, David had developed into a fierce warrior by fighting off both lion and bear when they came to attack the flock. I can only imagine how many times David practiced his slingshot out in those fields all by himself. Maybe he would set up his bag on a rock nearby and see how many times he could hit it with a rock, slowly perfecting his shot. Little did he know that the slingshot he carried around with him would one day be used to defeat the enemy of the living God.

David played his harp, wrote songs and Psalms to God, pouring out his heart to his heavenly Father. Did David ever know that his harp would lead him into the presence of King Saul, that he would provide the only relief Saul could find from the spirits that tortured his mind? Did David ever know that his Psalms, these raw, honest prayers to God, would be compiled within a book that would be placed within the canon of scripture?

> *Think about this: God takes the ordinary, mundane things in our life, and he uses them to shape us and our future. That's why we can't despise them, no matter how ordinary they may seem. We might never see or know just how these things will be used, but God does not waste our efforts or our obedience. God does not waste the little things that seem to have no real purpose. The seemingly insignificant thing in your hand today could be the very thing God chooses to use tomorrow.*

David could have easily despised the obscurity of the pasture, but he did not. He could have complained about getting the job nobody wanted, but instead he chose to train. He could have questioned God and his plans, but instead he chose to trust. He could have easily rejected the solitude of the pasture, but instead he saw it as preparation.

And what was David's motivation? I don't think it was the palace. I don't think he sat around daydreaming of the day when he would finally be the king. I'm not saying the thought didn't cross his mind a time or two, but, for David, the land of obscurity was not lost time or wasted time, it was a necessary part of the journey. It was foundational. It was about developing a passionate pursuit of God.

Much like many of the success stories that we hear today, David's success was the inevitable result of a long and arduous backstory played out in the land of obscurity. While many would say that the battle against Goliath was won in the Valley of Elah that day, David would probably tell you that the battle was won on the backside of a pasture a few miles away in the town of Bethlehem. Goliath was simply a formality. Goliath was the result of years of preparation.

Not only was the pasture a training ground, I believe it was a place of incredible joy for David. Our perspective on these in-between seasons can be the difference between a time of preparation and a time of restlessness. We can look back and see the hand of God in each and every part of our story, or we can live as though we have been forgotten or abandoned. The choice is up to us.

So, let me ask you a few very difficult questions. Are you embracing your obscurity, your pasture, or are you focused on where you want to be next? Are you despising the present situation because you believe you deserve something better or because you simply can't be "content" in your current place?

It's easy to get so focused on success and making an impact that our lives become more about what we're doing rather than about who we're becoming. We begin thinking that if we achieve enough, eventually it will bring what we're looking for. Spoiler alert: it doesn't. I hope you stick around and read through Part III: The Palace. Some people want to skip to that part of the book because that's the place most of us desire. But if we have not embraced the pasture and processed the cave moments in our life, the palace will never be enough. We can never just skip to the end in the story of our lives, and, in all honesty, we would miss out on all the beauty around us if we tried.

Take a lesson from one of the greatest kings and people of God who ever lived. Embrace the land of obscurity. Work your tail off when all the spotlights are off. Become a person of character and integrity when nobody is there to give you praise. Pursue a deep relationship with God first and foremost. Become addicted to the process and not the pat on the back. Follow David's example, and you may just find out that one day when Goliath does stand before you, it will be nothing more than another step in your process: the inevitable result of a deep relationship with God that has been forged in the land of obscurity.

Behind the Curtain

Turn on your TV or pull up a news website on any given day, and you will probably find the story of a leader or influencer who is now in the public eye for some sort of moral failure. We are often shocked to hear that people we've followed or greatly respected have their own darkness lying just below the surface. And yet, all of us to some extent are forced to wrestle with the implications of our own private and public lives. I'm not saying that everyone lives a life of duplicity or that immorality is justifiable, it's simply that we all have struggles we try to conceal from the general public or those around us. It's why Jesus asks us, "Why do you look at the speck of sawdust in your brother's eye and pay no attention to the plank in your own eye?" (Matthew 7:3). Even the question itself assumes that if we get close enough to an individual we will at some level be able to identify a "speck of sawdust" in their eye.

Although we may do our best to close the gap between our public life and private life, if we were one hundred percent honest, most of us would admit there are things we project in public that aren't consistent with our lives in private. In fact, some of the most public and vocal leaders are actually the most insecure in their private lives. They might have some sort of incredible ability or be a spectacular orator, but one attack or criticism sends them into a tailspin of doubt and insecurity.

This perfectly describes the life of Elijah. You would be hard pressed to find a more public or bolder encounter throughout the Bible than Elijah calling out King Ahab and the 450 prophets of Baal in 1 Kings 18. They gather on Mount Carmel, and the prophets of Baal begin to pray as Elijah only further taunts them. When they've prayed all day and nothing happens, Elijah moves into action. He builds an altar, and, just to increase the drama, he has twelve large jars of water poured over the offering that runs down into a trench surrounding the bull offering. In nothing less than a supernatural move of God, Elijah calls on God, and God sends his fire down at Mount Carmel to consume the sacrifice and all the water surrounding it.

Not only does Elijah experience this miracle, but he has the 450 prophets of Baal slaughtered. He then prophesies to King Ahab that the drought on the land is about to end; and God sends rain. Let me stop right here and say that anybody who experienced something like this would more than likely be experiencing an unprecedented spiritual high. 1 Kings 19 opens with these verses: "Now Ahab told Jezebel everything Elijah had done and how he had killed all the prophets with the sword. So, Jezebel sent a messenger to Elijah to say, 'May the gods deal with me, be it ever so severely, if by this time tomorrow I do not make your life like that of one of them.'"

Elijah just personally witnessed God perform public miracle after miracle after miracle, but Queen Jezebel made one threat toward his life, and here is Elijah's response: "Elijah was afraid and ran for his life. He came to a broom bush, sat down under it and prayed that he might die. 'I have had enough, Lord,' he said. 'Take my life; I am no better than my ancestors'" (1 Kings 19:3-4). But what could have possibly happened between chapters 18 and 19 that would have brought Elijah to this place of desperation? Is it possible that sometimes we can be a public success or project a certain confidence in front of others while struggling with our own demons just beneath the surface?

This may sound bizarre to some, but many of us understand this temptation all too well. I've led numerous small groups with pastors and church leaders over the years, and most of them can testify that often the greatest temptation or attack comes right after the greatest victory. It's the moments when you've seen God do something miraculous and you begin to descend from the mountaintop experience that you have to be the most aware. It was when "kings go off to war" in 2 Samuel 11:1 when David stayed behind and the temptation of Bathsheba ensued.

It can be one thing to project confidence and vision and passion when you are standing before the crowds, but it's an entirely different battle when you are alone, just staring in the mirror. This is why the hardest person you will ever lead will be yourself. If you can tame the soul staring at you in the mirror then there is no other person who will be able to throw you off course.

Deafening Silence

Nobody gives us a better picture of living in the tension of public notoriety and private solitude more than Jesus. In fact, the Bible only gives us a three-year glimpse into the life of Jesus. We can attempt to recreate the childhood of Jesus from what we know of history and the time period, but we are given very little in scripture. In fact, from age twelve to age thirty, we are only given one short verse in the Gospel of Luke. "And Jesus grew in wisdom and stature and favor with both God and man" (Luke 2:52). That's eighteen years of relative obscurity for three years of public ministry. That's 90 percent of your life preparing for about 10 percent of ministry.

And nobody seemed to value moments of isolation and solitude more than Jesus. In order to fulfill the will of the Father, Jesus knew that moments of isolation and renewal were absolutely mandatory. In fact, the Gospels give us several glimpses into the life of Jesus and how ministry seemed to always flow from these times of withdrawal. Mark 6 shows us a consistent theme that seems to identify the life of Jesus: Solitude to life to ministry.

Mark 6:

- Jesus goes to his hometown with his disciples, and they take offense at him and he leaves
- Jesus teaches and commissions his disciples
- John the Baptist is beheaded, and they receive the horrible news
- **Jesus takes the twelve to a quiet place to rest**
- The crowds find Jesus, and he feeds the five thousand through a miracle
- **Jesus dismisses the crowd, sends the disciples out on the lake, and retreats on the mountainside to pray**
- Jesus walks on the water to the disciples

> *Jesus had implemented the art of solitude and sabbath throughout his ministry. He was not defined by the crowds; he was defined by his relationship to the Father. If we plan on living like Jesus, then we better learn to listen and retreat like him.*

Obscurity also forces us to wrestle with our own solitude, a practice consistently overlooked in the lives of most leaders. Most leaders value characteristics such as productivity, fruitfulness, and activity. Solitude rarely makes the list because it seems counter-productive; an unnecessary value on the road to achieving our goals.

If a leader never embraces isolation and solitude, then they will never truly know who they are. Isolation is the great revealer. Not isolation that distances you from others, but isolation that forces you to look at yourself in the mirror and ask yourself the question, "Who am I?" Without these moments of determining our identity, we will inevitably cave to the opinions of others or take the easy road instead of the necessary road. Obscurity shows us who we are, stripped of our accolades, achievements, titles, and expectations. It's who we really are, not the person we want to be or the person we project to others. If people are put into places of leadership but they've never truly looked in the mirror, what emerges are leaders who will continually struggle with insecurity and only become what others want them to be.

Jesus had not only embraced the obscurity, but he also had learned how to be defined in his relationship with the Father. It defined him when he was unknown, and it defined him when the crowds began to push in to hear him speak. The solitude he practiced his entire life now defined the rhythms of his public ministry. This is another example of how greatness is never instantaneous but always the result of development over time.

I believe someone who is growing in spiritual maturity is learning to embrace solitude and isolation. These moments of solitude no longer leave us anxious or give us feelings of ineffectiveness. The silence is no longer deafening to us. Instead, they are moments we begin to crave; moments we can practice the art of being without the inward need to produce something for God or for others.

Dallas Willard, in his classic book *The Divine Conspiracy*, says this: "Solitude and silence give us a place to begin the necessary changes, though they are not a place to stop. They also give us some space to reform our inmost attitudes toward people and events. They take the world off our shoulders for a time and interrupt our habit of constantly managing things, of being in control or thinking we are in control. One of the greatest spiritual attainments is the capacity to do nothing. Thus, the Christian philosopher Pascal insightfully remarks, 'I have discovered that all the unhappiness of men arises from one single fact, that they are unable to stay quietly in their own room.'"[3]

Think about the implications of this quote by Pascal. The first time I heard it, I didn't really get it. The more I contemplated these words, the more I recognized the profound wisdom found in them. People who can sit quietly in their own rooms, without the need for any sort of external influence, have both control of what they do and what they don't do. There is nothing that has ultimate influence over them. They are slaves to nothing. They are not running to or from anything. Are you content to sit quietly in your own room without the need to go somewhere, do something, or find someone?

In 2008, the term "nomophobia" was coined to describe the irrational fear or anxiety disorder many people experienced when losing their mobile phone, being out of cell range, or running out of battery. The thought of not being connected or missing out on what may be happening creates anxiety in most people. Many of us can't go more than thirty minutes without checking something on our phone, and we can't imagine sitting alone somewhere in a waiting room or line without our phones there to steal our attention. Many of us are so insecure with ourselves that without a distraction or something to keep us occupied, we become incredibly uncomfortable.

We feed off the noise, the constant bombardment, the incessant drip of technology, news, travel and to dos. It becomes nearly impossible to sit alone in contemplation and meditation. But for the person who has learned to discipline themselves, to look deep into the silence and to embrace it, comes innumerable blessings and benefits.

Jesus was never controlled by the crowds or the agendas of others. He never got distracted by all the things and people and places that craved his affection and attention. In fact, there were numerous moments where he dismissed the crowds because the necessity of being alone with the Father was more important than the ministry that needed to be done. Let that sink in for a moment: Jesus left hurting people because he realized his capacity, he understood his limits, and he chose to minister out of the abundance of his time with the Father. Because he understood his calling and purpose, Jesus left towns where they clamored for him to return.

For years in ministry, I suffered from my own sort of messiah complex. I loved rescuing people and helping people, to the point that I would often let people take advantage of my time and resources. Early on in my marriage, my wife identified this problem, and she confronted me with the question, "Why do you allow people to do that to you?" My initial response was, "Because without me how would this person survive, or move forward, or walk in freedom, or get back on their feet?" I had embraced numerous lies but was blinded to see them until someone revealed them to me. My first lie was believing I was more important than I really was. That I could somehow play the role of God. My second lie was thinking that truly loving someone meant doing anything and everything necessary to keep them on the straight and narrow, even to my own personal detriment.

As a pastor, I've counseled hundreds of people throughout the years, and I've seen an emerging pattern. We often fail to set healthy boundaries with unhealthy people in our lives because we're afraid of the consequences or afraid of what may happen to them. We will drive ourselves into the ground or overwhelm ourselves with worry for the sake of someone else. It wasn't until I learned the importance of healthy boundaries that I understood that many times the most loving thing that I can do is to remain healthy myself. If I allow another person's dysfunction to become my own personal dysfunction, because I struggled to retain healthy boundaries, then I am no different than the person I'm trying to help. Without boundaries, we become slaves to the demands of those who surround us.

You can't lead out of your ability. You must learn to lead out of God's ability working in and through you. This is precisely why we must move from despising or neglecting solitude to craving it. We must be glaringly aware of our own personal weakness and inability, and, as a result, we will be able to stop long enough to listen, to hear, and to be filled once again.

Our American culture has successfully adopted a narrative that has unfortunately bled over into our theology. We live in such an egocentric, me-centered, my-way, status-conscious culture that we now believe it's our duty to create our identity. We take our experiences, our desires, others' opinions, and a myriad of other influences and we begin to develop our identity. The problem becomes that although these things should not be discounted altogether, they fail to provide a true plumb line for our identity. And now we have an entire culture looking to a younger generation screaming the message, "Follow your desires, your wants, and your natural proclivities."

> *But your identity was never meant to be created, it was meant to be discovered. What defines truth is not what a book tells us, but rather the character and nature of God, revealed in the person of Jesus Christ, and then given to us through scripture. So, truth is not first and foremost something God decides, but it is who he is;*

> *he cannot be separated from it. You cannot create your own brand of morality in the same way you cannot create your identity.*

God is just. God is love. God is good. As a result of his character and nature being revealed through Jesus and illuminated through scripture, you are deeply loved. You are valued. You are a son or daughter of God through faith.

Think about the implications of 1 John 4:7-8: "Dear friends, let us love one another, for love comes from God. Everyone who loves has been born of God and knows God. [8] Whoever does not love does not know God, because God is love." (NIV)

God is love. It's not an attribute he occasionally operates in, it's who he is. And if God is love, then in every moment and in every situation he is completely good and for you. This truth becomes not only the basis for God's character but also for your identity as someone who is deeply loved by God. That means that in the moment of obscurity when you aren't achieving anything and nobody knows your name and life seems to be passing you by—you are securely and deeply loved by the Father.

It is in our moments of solitude, accompanied by right thinking and understanding of who God is, that we begin to discover who we really are. The obscurity and the solitude allow us to see what otherwise we would never stop to see. They allow you to live with your eyes wide open. They allow us to remain centered no matter the circumstances of that day. And, ultimately, obscurity gives birth to identity: an inward certainty of who we are no matter what may be happening to us or around us.

CHAPTER 3

Detours in Disguise

Shortcuts

I'm sure you've been driving along at some point and started to see a sea of red brake lights in front of you. Immediately you begin trying to analyze the situation. Has there been a wreck? Is there a train stopped ahead? Is it a construction zone? You have just a few seconds to decide whether to wait in the line of traffic or to find an alternate route. If you can't tell by now, I absolutely hate sitting in traffic. And if you're wired like me, waiting is rarely an option. We would rather be moving somewhere, even if that means moving backwards. Movement is always progress, right? Well, not always.

I was once on church staff with an individual who absolutely refused to wait for passing trains. As soon as he would see the railroad lights begin to flash and the barricades begin to lower he would immediately bust a U-turn or look for the next side street. He absolutely refused to wait. I would say about 90 percent of the time his plan to cut through businesses, neighborhoods, and side streets added about five to ten minutes to our drive. In fact, it became almost comical to see him get so desperate to find a quicker route that he would be willing to drive through an open field in his Ford Explorer. The train had since passed, and all the cars had crossed the tracks, and there he'd be, still trying to find an alternate route. His "shortcuts" almost always turned into arduous detours.

Anytime we shortcut the process, we think we've taken a big move forward and we're one step closer to our destination. This is the irony of the shortcut. In reality, the shortcut always becomes a detour in disguise. You see, whatever we shortcut in our lives, we will eventually be forced to readdress. Think of it like this. If we're in mechanical school to become an air conditioner repairman, there are inevitably some ways that we can get around doing all the work. There are ways we can pass the test without knowing all the information. But one day we're going to be standing in front of an air conditioning unit that we are responsible for repairing. In that moment, it doesn't matter if we have a degree or that we passed an exam, the issue is whether or not we can fix the unit.

Please don't misunderstand me: this doesn't mean you turn a four-year degree into six or stay at a job twelve years when you only need eight. Don't let honoring the process become an excuse for inaction. But sometimes the only way to move forward is to wait. Sometimes the allure of progress will tell you to keep moving at all costs, but that movement isn't always productive. In fact, sometimes movement is a sign of your lack of faith. You believe you need to keep moving because if you don't then you'll never arrive at your destination.

As longtime leadership guru John Maxwell so pointedly put it: "There is a tendency in all of us to overestimate the event and underestimate the process. Every fulfilled dream occurred because of dedication to the process."[4] We want to get somewhere so quickly that we live our lives zoomed all the way in, thinking that all we need is the next thing to go right for us. When you zoom out and gain the clarity of perspective, you realize how the event was not nearly as significant as the bigger process.

Let me give you a glimpse of what happens when we shortcut the process. It's a story of a young man named Dustin who grew up in a Christian home. Dustin attended church, participated in all the youth activities, went on a short-term mission trip, and married a Christian girl two years after high school. Ten years into marriage and three children later, Dustin abandoned his wife for a woman he met at work. Everyone was horrified and bewildered. How could he be capable of this? Everything seemed to be just right. The reasons for such behavior are probably many, but I suspect that it's highly possible that somewhere along the way, Dustin shortcut or possibly even eliminated the process of character development. He stopped making the tough moral decisions that are so often necessary. He refused to keep his flesh in check and make himself accountable to the right people. He stopped fighting the fight. He stopped practicing the kind of faith that calls us to come and lay down our lives and our desires at the foot of the cross and walk in obedience. You see, shortcutting the process can have far more detrimental consequences than we are usually able to see in the moment.

It's why Jesus told a story about the wise and foolish builders (Matthew 7:24-27). Any decent builder will tell you that you've got to spend time, money, and effort getting the foundation right. If you cut corners or choose cheaper materials with the foundation, it doesn't matter how well you build the rest of the house, it will eventually crumble and fall.

As of 2019, the tallest building in the world is the Burj Khalifa Tower in Dubai, which stands 163 stories tall. It's truly amazing to see the process of laying a foundation for such a massive structure. They needed 192 massive steel pylons that were driven over 160 feet down into the rock below in order to sustain its infrastructure, which is nearly a half mile tall. The project began in January of 2004, and the process seemed slow at first because the average bystander couldn't see the more than 110,000 tons of concrete being poured below the surface. Once the foundation was set, the actual building began to go up rather quickly, and the project was completed and opened in January 2010. That is a lot of work without seeing any progress with the naked eye.

I'll never forget listening to a pastor I admired talk about the seasons of character development we go through. I was seventeen, and I had just recently felt called into ministry. I was starting to get opportunities to actually engage in ministry and even speak occasionally. I'll never forget him taking out a piece of paper and drawing a funnel, wide at the top and narrow at the bottom. He equated this funnel to the life of far too many pastors and leaders. We are heavy at the top with success or achievement and somewhat deficient at the bottom in character. We start to get addicted to the attention and pay less and less attention to our foundation. What happens to something that is extremely top-heavy with very little foundation? It inevitably tumbles over. What we see as waiting may just be the very thing God is trying to develop in us. I know for me that simple analogy has helped me embrace the process.

Unfortunately, every day we read headlines about people who shortcut the process. Maybe their success came too quickly. Maybe they thought that a position, a title, a certain amount of money, or other people's approval would somehow create the character or foundation that was lacking. I'll never forget listening to John Maxwell speak to a room full of church planters and ministry leaders about there being no shortcut for leaving a legacy. He said this about great leaders: "We may be used to instant oatmeal, coffee, and popcorn, but there's no such thing as an instant leader. Leadership is a crock-pot proposition that takes time, but in the end, it's always worth it. It ends up producing the kind of leaders that are worth following and that actually last." In our just-add-water culture, how difficult it can be for us to see beyond what is right in front of us. We easily forget that even the great men and women throughout the scriptures were forced to go the long way. For fifty years Abraham waited for the promise of an heir. Nearly forty years of Moses's life in Midian is described in one verse. Nearly eighteen years of Jesus's life is encapsulated in Luke 2:52. There is something important and necessary about taking the long way.

John Maxwell ended his message that day with a quote that still fuels me today: "And don't forget the longest distance between two points is always a shortcut."[5]

The Scenic Route

There's a story in scripture that can be pretty easy to skip right over. It's one of those back stories most people overlook that becomes the reoccurring tale of true "success" stories.

In a matter of a few years, David had gone from lowly shepherd to mighty warrior to one of the most successful generals of Israel's army. This rapid rise to fame aroused jealousy in the heart of Saul, and soon the great warrior David found himself a fugitive, constantly on the run from Saul and his pursuing army.

In 1 Samuel 26, Saul took his army down to the Desert of Ziph in order to seek out David and kill him. David and a few of his spies came across Saul's camp and saw Saul sleeping in the middle of the camp with his spear stuck in the ground right next to him. It seemed as though David was given the perfect opportunity to kill Saul and end this season of running for his life. To most people, killing Saul would not only have signified the end of David's fugitive journey, it also would have thrust him into position to become the next king over all of Israel. It's a no-brainer, right?

This scene wasn't even the first time David had been given the opportunity to kill Saul. Many would chalk this particular scenario up to fate. It must be that God wanted David to kill Saul and be done with all this running for his life. Even David's trusted warriors, one of his closest friends, told David, "Today God has delivered your enemy into your hands" (1 Samuel 26:8). So, what would you do if you were given the opportunity to end years of pain and begin a rocket-like journey toward success and promotion? What if you could justifiably end the only thing standing between you and your dream?

David's response was remarkable: "Don't destroy him! Who can lay a hand on the Lord's anointed and be guiltless? As surely as the Lord lives," he said, "the Lord himself will strike him; either his time will come and he will die, or he will go into battle and perish. But the Lord forbid that I should lay a hand on the Lord's anointed" (1 Samuel 26:9-11).

I've got to be honest. This response from David still floors me. Our culture today tends to have the belief that any open door must be a sign of God's will, so, to many of us, this would almost seem like the perfect invitation to move forward. It's just meant to be. Saul is trying to kill you and has been rejected by God as king, so you are fully justified in speeding up his exit and your promotion.

David, however, wouldn't take the bait. In that very moment when he ignored the shortcut in front of him, he knowingly took the longer route. Maybe it did make his journey longer. Maybe he did invite more pain and suffering into his life as he continued to run from Saul. Maybe he wouldn't see the palace for another ten years. I don't believe David saw his life like so many of us see our own. It wasn't just about becoming king, it was about honoring God and the authority God had instituted. It wasn't all about arriving at the so-called destination, it was about the journey God was taking him on. It's not just about becoming king; it's very much about how you got there.

More than that, look what David was really saying in his response: "It's ultimately not contingent on my efforts, but on God's will. If he desires me to be king over all of Israel, then God will remove Saul from his place of leadership, not me." What a picture of faith! What a picture of learning to truly trust that God is completely in control of all things. Think about it: this shows us that the pressure is off. Our calling is not based on our efforts or our will but on our obedience. God, who is completely and fully in control of all things, is not asking us to take out leaders or force our way into positions. God is asking us to walk in obedience, honor those in authority over us, and faithfully wait for God's timing.

If you're in an in-between season right now where you're not sure how it's going to work out, I hope you feel a weight lifted off your shoulders in this moment. You are not called to do the work that only God can do. Your good, loving Father is in full control of the situation, and your duty in this moment is faithfulness, obedience, and trust.

The Little Big Things

One of the measuring sticks for someone who has embraced the process is how they choose to handle the little things. When you're on the fast-track to success, there is no time for the little things. You become so obsessed with where you're going that there is no time to slow down and perfect the small details. But in God's process of promotion, the little things usually become the big things.

Over the past several years I've had the honor to assess, train, and coach many church planters. It's one of my greatest joys. One of the most difficult parts of this process is the assessment phase. It entails sitting down with an individual or couple and assessing their preparedness for the journey that lies ahead of them. I always tell these individuals my job is not to determine whether they are called (that's God's job), but whether they are prepared and have the gifting and skill set to be an effective church planter. Planting a church is a very difficult journey that requires incredible visionary capabilities, an exceedingly hard work ethic, and a certain level of spiritual and emotional maturity.

There are many individuals who sit before me on a regular basis wanting to lead a church, when they're not leading their spouse or family. They're ready to raise thousands of dollars for a new church plant, when their personal finances are in disarray. They're going to reach a city for Jesus, but they haven't personally shared Christ or discipled someone in years. For whatever reason, many people think that in the right circumstances they can just flip that switch and become excellent in those areas where they've previously lacked. Don't get me wrong, it's not about having all our ducks in a row or being complete in every area. If we wait for those moments, we stay in a continual holding pattern, never moving out. But we do see a pattern of preparation throughout the scriptures. Joshua does not go from completely inconspicuous and unknown, to God's man who will lead the people of Israel into the Promised Land. Joshua was by Moses's side in the wilderness, watching, learning, and preparing. He was next to the tabernacle as Moses walked inside to be in God's presence. Scripture even notes that Joshua lingered outside the tent of God's presence.

I've been extremely blessed to grow up in a home with amazing parents. As a young child, my family would have been considered a low-middle income family. My father worked for a local bank making very little, and my mother stayed at home with my sister and me. I watched over the years as my father was faithful to each and every job and slowly began climbing the ladder of leadership and management. When I was in middle school, my father stepped out on his own with two other individuals to start his own banking software company. In only a few years, that company would grow to over 300 employees, become one of *Inc. Magazine*'s fastest growing companies, and place my father in a position to be the national entrepreneur of the year (which he would eventually lose to Michael Dell of Dell Computers in their heyday). Today he oversees a missions organization with a vision to completely eradicate Bible poverty by 2030 through Bible translation. Many people will point to my parents' success or assume it's easier to be generous after you've experienced financial prosperity. For me, however, I remember growing up in a home where my parents were extravagantly generous before they ever experienced financial margin. I watched the faithfulness of my father in the small and seemingly mundane jobs before the awards and accolades ever started coming in. Most people want to point to his success or make assumptions from what they see, but I'm quick to point to the backstory, the long journey of doing the little big things that only happen in obscurity.

I planted my first church at a very young age. I felt somewhat unprepared and unqualified, but I knew the Holy Spirit was leading me to step out in faith. I was uncertain if I had what it took, so I went to several mentors and spiritual authorities, along with a church planting network, to confirm this calling. Since I was young, I always had other young men approach me who also were eager to jump into church planting. There was an allure and sexiness around church planting that made it seem like the trendy thing to do. I'll never forget one particular young man who approached me and was very inquisitive about planting his own church. We were just a few minutes into our conversation when I realized he wasn't connected to a local church at all. He wasn't actively being mentored by anyone, and he wasn't even serving or discipling others in any real capacity. He had these grand ideas of ministry, and yet somewhere along the way he had detached himself from what it looks like to be a healthy disciple of Jesus. He mentioned my young age when I first planted a church and my relative success as a church planter, and he assumed it could easily be replicated.

Over the next ten minutes I shared my story with him. I shared about the four years of interning, serving, and behind-the-scenes work done at a local church. The four years of ministry in college where I poured my life into young men for little to no compensation. I talked about the mentors and spiritual fathers who had surrounded me and provided me with a strong core from which I could launch. I ended our conversation with a very simple directive: Go back to your church home or find a church home with a godly leader and plant yourself there. Serve the body of Christ, and don't shortcut any part of that process. This particular young man did exactly what I requested, and today he is thriving in pastoral ministry. I wish all young men were like this young man, but they're not.

> *If God is truly more concerned with us that what we can do for him, he won't allow us to shortcut the process. He would never put us in a position where we aren't prepared for the test. Remember, God's tests are always designed to prepare, reveal, and build us, not to destroy us. The only time we find ourselves completely unprepared are the moments when we've chosen to shortcut or neglect the place we're in.*

Our hearts are always revealed in the little things, the small details. Do we give out of our need or only in our abundance? Do we honor someone in a position of authority even when they're wrong or we don't agree with them? Do I give 100 percent in a class that seems to have no real impact on my future? Will I love and serve someone who can do nothing for me in return? How do I handle a job that is far from my dreams and desires? Am I good steward of the little I've been given?

It's in the small, big things that our heart and motives are revealed.

Revealed by Fire: A Parable

Once there was a great king who was distinguished beyond all others in the land and was known for his amazing skill in battle. A great royal feast was being prepared to honor the king and his men as they prepared for war. In this land, nothing was considered more sacred and honorable than those who fought for their people. The king bore the sole responsibility for his men and the outcome of the war. It was tradition in the land for the king to be presented with a new sword, which he would use to lead his men into battle. Several weeks before the great feast, the king selected two well-respected blacksmiths to craft the very sword he would use to defeat the enemy. The two men would present their swords before the king, but only one of them would be chosen. One blacksmith would be greatly honored and be given the opportunity to sit at the right side of the king during the feast, while the other would receive nothing.

One week before the swords were to be presented, the king asked his young son to go and watch the two blacksmiths as they worked. He said nothing more to the young boy than to go and observe the two blacksmiths' every move and report back to him at the end of the week. The young boy must also make sure that neither blacksmith knew they were being watched. Each day for a week, the young boy secretly watched the men through the knots in the wood. He careful observed their every movement. Neither blacksmith had any notion that they were being watched as they carefully crafted their swords for the king.

The first blacksmith spent innumerable hours heating and reheating the iron to the exact temperature. On many occasions, he would discard the entire piece of metal and start over again. With intricate maneuvering and delicate adjustments, he forged and shaped the blade to absolute perfection. As the sweat poured from the face of the blacksmith, he worked tirelessly to bring the blade to completion and to create a hilt that was both strong and comfortable. Although the sword consisted of nothing but iron and leather, its overall structure was essentially flawless.

While the first blacksmith was perfecting his sword, the second blacksmith was traveling all throughout the region searching frantically for the finest jewels and the most ornamented golden trinkets. It was his desire to craft a sword unlike any other of its kind. When the second blacksmith returned from finding these precious items, he quickly forged a sword much like he had done a thousand times before. The hilt of this sword, however, was lavished with gold-plated emblems and rubies that could only be seen in the hands of a king. The hilt alone consumed almost the entire focus of the blacksmith. While the blade was slightly unbalanced and the iron not heated to exact perfection, these slight imperfections were undetectable to the naked eye and were quickly overlooked by the splendor of its appearance.

The final day had approached and the two men stood in front of the throne as they presented their swords before the king. With great joy and pride the second blacksmith uncovered his sword from the lavish box and rotated it in the light so that its beauty could be seen from every angle. The rubies and emeralds cast against the gold-plated hilt created an explosion of light, which reflected off the bricked walls of the palace. The first blacksmith slowly and reverently uncovered the sword from its burlap wrapping and gently laid it at the feet of the king. While there were no brightly decorated aspects to the sword, it was apparent that the sword was crafted to fulfill its purpose.

The first blacksmith knelt before the king and kept his eyes focused on the ground below him, as his hard, calloused hands clutched the burlap sack that had covered the sword. The second blacksmith remained standing and gave forth an air of complete confidence. The two men waited in eager anticipation for the king to make his choice. Instead of choosing between the two swords, however, the king turned to his young son standing in the corner and motioned for him to come. As the young boy emerged from the corner of the room, the king looked at him and said, "You decide which of these swords I will use to lead my men into battle.

The king understood that his son had seen the work of both men when they thought nobody was watching. The young boy had seen the intricate details of each man's work and the time put into each sword. Only this boy would know which sword would be worthy of battle. The king believed the young man to be the perfect age, because he was intelligent enough to know when something was made with excellence, and yet innocent enough not to be clouded by issues such as greed and pride.

The young boy, with a sense of apprehension, looked up into the eyes of his father, the king. With great care, the young boy walked over to the first blacksmith's sword and picked it up off the ground. He clutched the sword with both hands and held it out in front of him, as his eyes slowly traveled down the edge of the sword. The young boy then proceeded to hand the sword to his father. The dull, gray appearance of the sword created a significant contrast against the flowing, velvet robe of the king. As the king's fingers slid down the smooth, polished blade, he immediately realized that the sword was crafted with an excellence and diligence unlike any he had ever seen. It was truly a sword worthy for battle.

The king looked down at the young boy and asked him, "Why did you choose this sword, my son?" The boy looked back at the king and replied, "Because, father, I don't care how you look as you long as you come back home after the battle."

He looked down at the young boy and gave him a quick nod of assurance as he took the leather strap from his waist and fastened the sword to his side. Seeing that he had done his job, the young boy quickly turned and proceeded down the stairs of the palace entrance. From there the king turned and looked to the first blacksmith and motioned for him to come and follow him into the dining hall. As the king and the first blacksmith walked through the palace halls and into the dining room, the second sword lay there, untouched, before the throne.

CHAPTER 4

The Art of Being

Hamster Wheels

Years ago, I heard a story that continues to resonate in my soul. Imagine a dad taking his oldest son on a camping trip. That evening as they're sitting around the campfire, he looks at him and tells him, "Son, I want you to know what I want from you in your life. I want you to be the very best at everything you do. I want you to graduate with honors, get a scholarship to a prestigious university, get a great job, and be a success in life."

What do you think his son would seek to do the rest of his life? If he's anything like the majority of us, he's going to leave the campfire that evening and spend the rest of his life trying to earn the approval of his father through his accomplishments. The only problem is that it will more than likely never be enough and will produce a deep-seated insecurity that only comes through basing his life off his performance. It's never enough. It's like running on a hamster wheel and hoping to get somewhere, or getting dropped in the middle of the Pacific Ocean and being told, "Swim to shore!" It's pointless.

And yet most of are perfectly content living our lives on the treadmill of performance, going faster and faster and yet never getting any closer to what we're searching for. Maybe we choose to do this because we don't know another way. Maybe we do this because we are achievers who get our sense of self-worth from our accomplishments. But maybe we are doing this because we fundamentally misunderstand how our heavenly Father sees us.

Let me paint another scenario for you. Imagine that while this father and his son are sitting around the campfire, the father says, "Son, I want you to know the one thing I want from you in your life. No matter what happens, good or bad, whether we agree or disagree, no matter what you do or where you go, I SIMPLY WANT TO KNOW YOU. I want to have a relationship with you just like we have right now sitting around this fire." What sort of transformation happens within the heart of his son that night?

> *Here's what we must understand about God. While the Father will rejoice in our life accomplishments, his love for us is unconditional. We are loved, period. That may seem small and simple, but it changes absolutely everything to know that God doesn't fall in or out of love with us or that his affection doesn't rise or fall depending on our performance over the last week. The implication of this truth is that, in every place and in every season, we never have to question the love of the Father on our behalf. In that moment, the son experiences an unconditional love and grace in which he can truly rest.*

In case you didn't know, or if you're like me and need a constant reminder, our heavenly Father is sitting around the campfire calling us to relationship with him. Not based on our past, our failures, or our qualifications; but based solely on his love and grace. Grace that when fully realized will profoundly change our life.

So, is God's purpose to bring us to some sort of calling, or is it to know him? How we answer this question will determine much about our understanding of God. This becomes a major tension that anyone who follows Jesus must learn to manage. I believe the story of David lives in this tension. Samuel came looking for God's next anointed, the man who would guide Israel to become the nation God intended. This calling, however, was dependent on a certain characteristic that the next king must possess: the right heart. God was not looking for the next talent or the most gifted person or even the man who looked the part. He was looking for a leader who understood submission, humility, and intimacy. The characteristics that only develop when one is focused on the art of "being" with God. The discipline of learning to "abide" and "remain" connected to the vine.

As Robert Clinton puts it, your second-order calling will only emerge if you have first embraced your first-order calling. In other words, the things that God has called you to "do" will only be a direct result of your ability to "be" with him.

Your first-order calling is simply God's invitation to live in a relationship of loving intimacy with God through the redemption of the cross and acceptance of the lordship of Jesus. And God will never skip over your first-order calling in order to arrive at your second-order calling. Your second-order calling is God's invitation to follow him in service in the world, using our spiritual gifts for his glory.[6] You experience this second-order calling as a "spillover" or "overflow" of someone who is living in their first-order calling.

A Revelation of Grace

I was in my second year of full-time ministry as a college/young adult pastor at a growing church. I was also finishing up a graduate degree in theological studies. After seven years of theological studies I was ready for a break, and I could see the end in sight. I needed one more elective credit and decided to take a spiritual formation course; not because I necessarily felt I needed it, but because it was a two-week class with a set reading list and one major paper. It seemed like the quickest route to finishing my degree. Little did I know how that week would shape my life.

We had a guest professor for the course who couldn't care less about our grades, but who was determined to birth a deeper desire for God in our hearts. He began taking us through a series of spiritual formation practices such as Lectio Divina, listening prayer, and abiding prayer; these were practices I had learned before but had never practiced on a regular basis. We began delving into the spiritual formation classics and mystics who had helped shaped our understanding of God and spiritual growth over the centuries. This journey began to uncover some deep issues in my heart. I began to see idols I had allowed to develop over the years, justifying them for the cause of ministry or achievement or productivity. I began to see how clouded my heart had become and how I struggled with resting in God's grace and love. I couldn't just sit, I needed to be doing something, I needed to be going somewhere.

One particular afternoon we were practicing a Lectio Divina exercise, a process of slowly and prayerfully reading a story. The text was on Martha and Mary in Luke 10. During this time of prayer and solitude, I finally came face-to-face with my struggle. It was almost as though I could picture myself in the story, busily working in the kitchen trying to achieve enough to be counted worthy. I had a faulty, underdeveloped understanding of grace and what it meant to live and rest in that love. Growing up in my particular denominational background, we occasionally talked about grace, but only after we thoroughly discussed the discipline of living a life of holiness. And holiness was never discussed in the context of God's love or goodness for us, but always in a way that left me trying to play catch-up.

Life, ministry, and my relationship with Christ had become a chore, a means to an end, a tireless trudge to build a ministry that was reaching people for Jesus. I had become distracted and lost focus of my true primary calling. I could see Jesus saying to me what he was saying to Martha that day: "Stop, walk away from the kitchen, and just sit with me. We'll go back to the kitchen later, but with joy, not burned out by life. Matt, you are not what you do. Matt, you are more important to me than the ministry you provide. Matt, lay down your performance mentality and walk into my grace." I made a shift that week. I began to understand grace in a way that radically changed my relationship with him. Twenty-four years into life and I got my first real revelation of grace that would forever change how I understand God and my relationship with him.

It was like a breath of fresh air to my soul. It wouldn't happen overnight, but as I began to lean into this understanding of grace, years and years of performance-based religion began to surface. A sobering realization that I had become more like the Pharisees in the story and Jesus was gently inviting me into something so much better, something that wouldn't fluctuate based upon how much I achieved. I could actually be Mary without guilt or condemnation or a feeling that I was being lazy. Jesus was not only allowing it, but inviting me into it. This was how he designed it to be from the beginning, but sin and death had fractured the beauty of that grace-driven communion with the Father.

Here's another sobering lesson I learned during that time: I had lost the awe and wonder of sitting at the feet of Jesus.

> *When you lose your fascination with Jesus, you will seek that fascination in something else. That something else, whether overtly good or evil, will inevitably become your idol. Sometimes this can take the form of an addiction or a relationship, but it can often take the form of "good things" that are not the "primary things." It can take the form of ministry or helping others or social justice issues or building the next business: good things we become fascinated with more than him.*

The isolation, the obscurity, the solitude allows us to see what otherwise we would never stop to see. If we don't learn the rhythms of slowing, silence, and being, then we will inevitable get caught up in the current of performance. Slowing is the art of pulling ourselves back to center when everything around us is pulling us away and telling us, "You are what you accomplish! You are what others say you are! You are what you've struggled with!"

Let me be honest. This has been one of the greatest revelations in my life, and yet it continues to be one of my greatest struggles. The constant pull of achievement and the list of things that still need to be done constantly try to hijack the love the Father wants me to experience in relationship with him.

Years ago, with the help of a spiritual formation coach and mentor, I began to develop a clearer understanding of my natural tendencies and developed a plan to be proactive, not reactive. I began to identify ways in which the enemy deceives me or attempts to hijack my understanding of God and my identity in him. I discovered that oftentimes I would neglect extended times in solitude or prayer because I felt guilty for not being productive or felt that I couldn't waste my time when I should be working. It was only after these discoveries and replacing the lies I had believed with the truth that I began to shift in my thinking and my lifestyle.

I learned how to observe the Sabbath. I learned how to retreat. I learned replenishing activities that renewed my mind, body, and spirit. I learned that there is too much at stake to not stop and slow down. That if I was going to lead myself, my wife, my children, and my church and finish well, I had to learn the art and rhythms of solitude and of a relationship with Christ not predicated on myself or my efforts, but on him and on my standing as a son. There has been nothing that has transformed my life and faith more than living in this revelation of God's grace. I can honestly say it has given me my true identity.

There is simply no substitute for the pasture. Like David, it becomes the foundation from which our life journey takes shape. It forms us, shapes us, and prepares us for what we cannot even begin to know. David entered the pasture young, naïve, and ill-equipped, but he would leave the pasture matured, developed, and positioned for what God was about to do next. Although the day-after-day routine may have seemed rather ordinary and insignificant something was happening just below the surface that would affect his life, his family, a nation, and generations after him.

What does your pasture look like today? Is it getting passed over for the promotion you thought you deserved? Is it being single? Is it a medical diagnosis? Is it numerous delays that have kept you from pursuing your dream? Is it being in a job, city, or situation you didn't expect or didn't want? It may not be easy or what you anticipated, but let me challenge you to lean in. It's not "if" God is up to something, but "what" God is up to and how this season of life is shaping you. And maybe, just maybe, if you stop long enough to embrace the place you're in, you will begin to see the beauty that God brings in the most unlikely of places.

PART II: THE CAVE

> *"God has a university. It's a small school. Few enroll; even fewer graduate. Very, very few indeed. God has this school because he does not have broken men and women. Instead, he has several other types of people. He has people who claim to have God's authority...and don't – people who claim to be broken...and aren't. And people who do not have God's authority, but who are mad and unbroken. And he has, regretfully, a great mixture of everything in-between. All of these he has in abundance, but broken men and women, hardly at all. - A Tale of Three Kings* by Gene Edwards

There are moments in life when we find ourselves in the pasture, seemingly miles away from our destination and defined by times of obscurity and solitude. There are other moments we never saw coming that send us into a tailspin of doubt and uncertainty. They are usually moments that test everything we have and even cause us to question whether God is involved; whether we really heard his voice or whether there is a plan for our lives. "Shouldn't it be just a little bit easier if God is really behind all this?" We end up believing that our current circumstances are an accurate gauge for whether God is with us or in this. God may seem distant, the calling gone or at least delayed, and the vision for how we saw our lives transpiring is dead.

In 1 Samuel 22, David found himself in a place he never dreamed, a place of pain he had been thrust into through a series of life events. David escaped from the hand of Saul and went wandering into the desert only to wind up in the Cave of Adullum all alone. I believe Adullum represents rock bottom. It is the place where the call and even the faithfulness of God is called into question. It represents those moments where it "wasn't supposed to go like this." Your story wasn't supposed to be this difficult. If David was really supposed to be the next king over all of Israel, wouldn't he catch a few more breaks along the way?

Adullum can also represent the brokenness of this world. The pain of losing a loved one. The pain of betrayal. The pain of watching a child, friend, loved one walk down a path of darkness. Whatever the situation, Adullum is the place none of us want to experience but each of us will at some point in our lives. Jesus never denied the reality of suffering in this world. In fact, he comes straight out and confirms it and attaches it to the hope of eternity that brings us comfort in the midst of the trial. "In this world you will have trouble, but take heart, I have overcome the world" (John 6:33).

In one moment, David, the great warrior and musician, was playing his harp for the king, and in the next moment he was kissing his wife goodbye and climbing out a side window to save his life (1 Samuel 19:2). Next, living like a fugitive, he ran to Nob, where Ahimelech the priest was stationed. Ahimelech asked the question any of us would ask if we saw the vice president of the United States walk into our business or church completely alone: "What are you doing here? Why are you alone? Aren't you always accompanied by an entourage of security and secret service or something like that?"

In desperation, David took the consecrated bread as food and asked for the only weapon around: the sword David himself had used to kill Goliath. How very fitting! The very sword that had been enshrined into the Israelite museum of history to display God's faithfulness would now be the very sword David would need to defend himself in his greatest test to date.

Goliath's sword is just another example to show us that God does not waste anything. Things in our hands today can be just what we need tomorrow. He will never waste our victories, successes, failures, mountaintops, or valleys—and this is the essence of redemption. We may not always see the significance or purpose in the plan, but God will always use our experiences and his process to lead us where he is calling us to go. When David stood before the whole Philistine army holding Goliath's sword up as a symbol of Yahweh's triumph, he never would have guessed that in just a few years he would need more faith than ever and that very sword to protect him from his own king.

From Nob, David traveled to Gath, where, out of fear for his life, he pretended to be mad so King Achish would let him go free. After Gath, David traveled further into the desert and stopped at the Cave of Adullum. In the life of David, it's important we stop to understand the gravity of the Cave of Adullum. It represents the place where the calling, expectations, frustrations, doubts, and fears converged. It's the place where, just like David, we will be forced to wrestle with the deepest part of our faith and character. It's the place where we will consider letting go of the dream God has placed deep within our hearts. It represents the place of our deepest pain, our deepest fears, and our deepest uncertainties and confusion. It is the epitome of the place where our dreams and God's plan seem to be in opposition.

This low point is also the place where God can do the deepest soul work. It's in the cave where we learn the painstaking process of SURRENDER. It's painful, it's uncomfortable—it's also absolutely indispensable in God's process. If a Christian never comes to his or her Cave of Adullum, then he or she will inevitably hold onto pieces of their lives, or at least the outcomes. Only when we see the shattered pieces of our plans and agendas sitting in a pile over in the corner do we learn that living by faith is more about trusting in him than it is about figuring out our future. Please don't get me wrong: you have a very real decision to make when you're in the cave. It's just as easy to become bitter, cynical, and disillusioned as it is to become surrendered. In fact, it's in the cave where many people choose to blame God and the enemy deceives them into believing false truths about God's nature and character.

I know it sounds rather pessimistic, but I once heard a wise person say, "You're either headed into your cave, currently in the middle of your cave, or on your way out of the cave." I've realized this is true. Let's not forget this is not David's only stop on the road to surrender and brokenness. You could also read about David in Ziklag (1 Samuel 30), or the infamous David and Bathsheba story (2 Samuel 11), or how David fled after his son Absalom came for the throne (2 Samuel 15), or how David was punished for his disobedience in taking a census (2 Samuel 24).

But Adullum was the first major experience of brokenness in David's life, and something incredible happened that day at Adullum. In 1 Samuel 22, in the depth of David's despair, his family and a group of misfit bandits came to the cave to rally around David. It's not exactly the group of people David had anticipated leading. David assumed the future king over Israel would attract a different crowd, but sometimes you take what God gives you. Now David found himself the accidental leader of a group of outsiders who didn't belong and had nowhere else to go. Those with criminal pasts, the outlaws, the marginalized, and those who were just downright discontent with their life. It wasn't exactly what David had envisioned, but let's be honest—it never is. We automatically assume that it's God's plan B, but who's to say it wasn't his plan A. Again, I guess it's all about how you come to see your journey of faith. God uses the "cave" to once again refine our hearts and redefine our expectations. It may seem like the place of loneliness, defined by discouragement and abandonment, but those are the moments when we are most positioned to have a transformative encounter with God.

If you're in a cave, I'm not saying it will be easy, and you will more than likely be tempted to let go of your calling, dream, or future. Or you can embrace the deep soul work God does in the cave. Take heart knowing he is right in the middle of your darkest hour.

The pasture has taught us IDENTITY. Let's see how the cave can teach us the indispensable act of SURRENDER.

CHAPTER 5

Emptied

Empty Containers

As a parent, I've learned that pain is often the great educator for my children. I can tell them a hundred times not to get close to the edge of the fire pit in our backyard because it's so hot, and yet they still get a few inches away. A few years ago, my youngest son, Jude, simply forgot about steel edge of the fire pit and reached out and grabbed it to steady himself from falling. Needless to say, I've never had to remind him again.

I've learned that, just like my children, as an adult I often learn my greatest spiritual lessons through pain. Honestly, I wish there was a better way. Most of the time our emptying only comes through brokenness: intense moments of wounding when we loosen the grip on our lives and wholeheartedly cling to him. But why is brokenness often only brought about through suffering? Why can't we learn these same lessons through victory, mountaintops, and successes?

The human heart is fickle and unpredictable. It is capable of incredible goodness, and, at other times, full of immense pride and rebellion. It's the moments of brokenness that draw our hearts to him, while so often it's the victories that swell our hearts with arrogance and pride. Our hearts bestow glory upon ourselves when we believe our victories are based on our own gifts and abilities and not God's mighty work in us.

That's why I'm fully convinced that all of God's chosen servants walk with a limp. Can you imagine being Jacob? Can you imagine walking the rest of your life with a visible limp? Every step you take you are reminded of this encounter, and every person you meet asks the question, "What happened?" You continually, even daily, recount the struggle of wrestling with God—the struggle that persisted all through the night. How that must have shaped Jacob for a lifetime! That must have led him to a place of surrender each time he took a step!

Too often we assume God is looking for someone who is complete and put together, when in reality he must empty us before he can fill us. God cannot fill what is already occupied, and there is so much that occupies our hearts. He must chip away all the "me" we have built up inside us until we truly become empty. An empty container says, "God, fill me as you choose," while full containers desire God to use them as they are and according to their own ways. Are you planning your future and asking God to bless it, or are you fully submitting yourself to his plans?

Think about the following scenarios:

- Moses fled to the desert—after killing an Egyptian
- Jacob wrestled with God—after cheating his brother of the birthright
- Joseph sat in a prison cell—after being falsely accused of rape
- Abraham raised the knife—after being told to murder his son
- Elijah ran into the desert—after being overrun with fear by Queen Jezebel
- David came to the cave—after running for his life from King Saul

What do each of these scenarios have in common? There was a letting go. There was a moment when they had no choice but to let go of their expectations, dreams, plans, and ideas and learn to fully trust in God. In the letting go there are usually more questions than answers, and each of us is forced to lean in when our minds and flesh are saying, "This can't be his plans."

If we don't have moments when we fully trust him and where there are no safety nets or plan B's, then we will never fully learn to trust him with everything. We will always keep back a portion of ourselves from him. That is also the portion that will usually come back around to be the un-surrendered, un-yielded part of our lives where idols are crafted.

The emptying is rarely pleasant. While some of us may choose to live broken before God, many of us will only come to this level of brokenness through events in our lives. When our comforts, our idols, and our understandings are ripped from us, we are often drawn back to him in a profound way. In that moment we come face-to-face with our own limitations. We understand those things, people, or ideas in which we placed our hope and security are, in fact, fleeting and completely incapable of providing an anchor for our souls amidst the storms of life. These moments may be painful for us to navigate, but they are essential to our souls. We need constant and consistent reminders that nothing else in our lives can provide the hope we need apart from him.

In his book *The Return of the Prodigal*, Henri Nouwen expounds on the parable in Luke 15 where the younger son takes half of his father's estate and goes to a foreign land to squander all of it on wild living. Nouwen notes that the younger son doesn't reclaim his "sonship" until everything has been lost. "He hit the bedrock of his sonship. In retrospect, it seems that the prodigal had to lose everything to come into touch with the ground of his being."[7] At the bottom of his despair, the younger son stares at the food being consumed by the pigs, and his physical hunger overtakes him. His physical despair led him to a reality of his spiritual despair. I often wish these realizations could come a different way, but how difficult it can be for God to grab the attention of someone who has already decided their path.

Where will our stories go next? We know that we will inevitably face times of pain and suffering in our lives. Will we wait for life to break us or will we choose to live a life of constant brokenness before him?

Please don't misunderstand: The cave was never a place where God crushed his leaders; it was the place where he emptied them. It wasn't God's plan that they would walk around the rest of their days feeling defeated or overwhelmed by the brokenness they were facing. The cave, in hindsight, was always a place of surrender, not destruction. As Ann Voskamp so beautifully says: "It is not through our success that God saves the world, but through our sacrifice. He calls us first to an altar, not a platform."[8] What would happen if we all sought after fewer platforms and more altars?

Humility Magnets

The cave is also the place where humility is driven deep into the hearts of God's people. And humility may be the very characteristic that turns God's head toward us more than anything. If God stands in complete opposition to pride, isn't it also true that God fully embraces the humble (1 Peter 5:5)? That he is looking for humble people who have embraced the obscurity of the pasture and surrendered their agendas in the cave?

The issue is not if pride exists in our hearts, but where and how it is being expressed in our lives. If pride is not continually laid at the altar of surrender, then it will inevitably surface in how we lead others. As we discussed earlier in the book, King Saul made many mistakes. In 1 Samuel 15, Saul was instructed by the prophet Samuel to completely destroy the Amalekites for what they had done to Israel years earlier. There was nothing of the Amalekites that would be spared. Instead, Saul chose to keep King Agag as a prisoner along with the best of the sheep, cattle, fat calves, and lambs—"everything that was good" (1 Samuel 15:9). That's important, but in my opinion it's not the most appalling point of the story. God was grieved that he made Saul king, so early in the morning Samuel left to find Saul. When Samuel arrived, he was told, "Saul has gone to Carmel. There he has set up a monument in his own honor and has turned and gone on down to Gilgal" (1 Samuel 15:12).

Saul was gone. The king was down at Carmel making a monument *in his own honor*. Not a monument or altar dedicated to God, to thank him for providing their victory in battle, but an altar to commemorate what Saul had accomplished in this victory.

> *Pride will not only keep us from complete obedience, it also will be quick to grab the spotlight. If we are not fully surrendered, then we will inevitably take the credit and assume that the victories in front of us are a result of our giftedness and not his grace and goodness.*

Even Jesus's disciples struggled with this reality. I've always thought it somewhat unfair how the Gospel of Mark depicts the disciples. In Mark's Gospel, this group of twelve constantly got it wrong, misunderstood almost every situation, and perpetually failed to live up to the expectations around them. They were honestly depicted as a group of bumbling idiots. Nothing depicts this more than Mark 9-10, where Jesus radically redefined the concept of greatness. In Mark 9, Jesus confronted the twelve disciples about their argument on the road regarding who was the greatest in the kingdom of God. In Mark 10, Jesus corrected their false assumptions that they could sit to his right and left in the kingdom of heaven. There was a total and radical reconstructing of how we must now view life, leadership, and greatness.

"And Jesus called them to him and said to them, 'You know that those who are considered rulers of the Gentiles lord it over them, and their great ones exercise authority over them. But it shall not be so among you. But whoever would be great among you must be your servant, and whoever would be first among you must be slave of all. For even the Son of Man came not to be served but to serve, and to give his life as a ransom for many'" (Mark 10:42-45).

This signals a turning of everything on its end. We now have to flip how we view greatness and see it through the lens of the kingdom of God, rather than the kingdom of this world.

God is undoubtedly drawn to the humble. You could say that humility operates as a magnet, drawing both the attention of God and others around us. We feel an innate pull toward individuals who, although they may possess high levels of talent, decide to elevate the status of those around them above their own.

Every year our church would host a large youth convention attended by thousands of teenagers from across the state. As a junior and senior in high school, I served as transport for the guest speakers we would invite to speak. I remember hand washing my 1998 two-door Chevy Tahoe and vacuuming the inside to make sure it was spotless. I put on a dress shirt and slacks and made sure I was at the airport at least thirty minutes early so they wouldn't have to wait for a single second. I had a bottled water ready for them in the cup holder, with mints and the day's schedule on the seat. It was exciting for me because I would get about twenty-five minutes of one-on-one time with these incredible men of God as I drove them from the airport to the church and made arrangements for their dinner and hotel that evening.

I was responsible for two speakers that week, and I'll never forget those two individuals. My first speaker was Matthew Barnett, pastor of Angelus Temple in Los Angeles and co-founder of the Dream Center. My second guest was Joe White, founder and president of Kanakuk Kamps. From the moment Matthew and Joe got into my car, they didn't stop asking me about my life, my activities, and my faith. I remember Matthew Barnett handing me his business card with his personal contact information and insisting I come out to the Dream Center in LA this summer. I remember Joe White stopping and talking to an eight-year-old young boy as we were walking into the church. Most people would have walked right on by and would have never even noticed. Not only did Joe stop, but he took the time to really listen to the young boy and gave him 100 percent of his attention. I immediately knew why Kanakuk Kamps had such an incredible reputation. It trickled down from the very top.

As I listened to them preach, the power of their sermons was only enhanced by my experience of them offstage. Their humility and genuine love of people impacted me more than what they preached that day. In fact, I honestly don't remember what they preached, even though I'm sure it was great. I will, however, never forget my short time with them in the car and my conversations with them. I will never forget their humility and the way they showed value for each person they met.

The proud will usually do whatever is necessary to climb the ladder of success. They always have an agenda and are continually leveraging others for their own benefit. They are determined to get the position, gain the notoriety, and vault themselves to the front without much consideration of who or what stands in their way. Pride often leads us to ask the question, "Why am I doing this?" if there is nobody there to praise our efforts or we don't receive the satisfaction of public applause.

But those who are humble in heart have changed the rubric for success. The humble have wrestled with who they are and who God has called them to be. They no longer need to climb the ladder to gain their identity since it is now deeply rooted in being a blessing, not receiving the blessing. They value people for who they are and do not use them as a stepladder. They allow God to be their promoter and do not need to make it happen through their own pushing or striving. They are servants because greatness is not found in the number of followers or the size of their audience. They have found peace with who they are.

Years ago, I heard a story about a young man's encounter with a reputable preacher and theologian.

In 1966 the young man joined Operation Mobilization (OM), a missions organization focused on training and mobilizing young missionaries across the globe. He was planning on serving for a year in France, but spent two years in India instead. While in London that summer, at the one-month OM orientation, he decided to volunteer to work on a cleanup crew late one night.

Around 12:30 a.m., the young man was sweeping the front steps of the conference center when an older gentleman approached and asked if this was the OM conference. He told him it was, but almost everyone was in bed.

The older gentleman had a small bag with him and was dressed very simply. He said he was attending the conference, so the young man said, "Let me see if I can find you a place to sleep." Since there were many different age groups at OM, he thought he was an older OMer. He took him to the room where he had been sleeping on the floor with about fifty others, and, seeing that the older gentleman had nothing to sleep on, laid some padding and a blanket on the floor and used a towel for a pillow. The older gentleman said it would be fine and that he appreciated it very much.

As he was preparing for bed, the young man asked him if he had eaten. He had not because he had been traveling all day. He took him to the dining room, but it was locked. So, after picking the lock, he found cornflakes, milk, bread, butter, and jam—all of which he appreciated very much. As the older gentleman ate, they began to fellowship, and the young man asked where he was from. He said he and his wife had been working in Switzerland for several years in a ministry mainly to hippies and travelers. When he finished eating, they all turned in for the night.

However, the next day the young man found himself in big trouble! The leaders of OM really got on the case of this young man. "Don't you know who that man is on the floor next to you?" they asked. "It is Dr. Francis Schaeffer, the speaker for the conference!" The young man did not know they were going to have a speaker, nor did he know who Francis Schaeffer was, nor did he know they had a special room prepared for him!

After Francis Schaeffer became well-known because of his books, and the young man had read more about him, he thought about this occasion many times—this gracious, kind, humble man of God sleeping on the floor with OM recruits! This was the kind of man he wanted to be.

Why is God drawn toward humility? Why is it that the face of God is turned toward the humble in heart? Look no further than Philippians 2:5-8:

"In your relationships with one another, have the same mindset as Christ Jesus: Who, being in very nature God, did not consider equality with God something to be used to his own advantage; rather, he made himself nothing by taking the very nature of a servant, being made in human

likeness. And being found in appearance as a man, he humbled himself by becoming obedient to death—even death on a cross!"

Why is God drawn toward the humble? It seems as though we are never more like Jesus than when we are willing to make ourselves nothing and to exalt those around us. When we give away the applause instead of receiving it and choose to go unnoticed rather than taking the attention. This is living proof that gospel transformation has taken place in our hearts. We no longer need the credit or desire the spotlight because he is already enough for us. In a world where we are addicted to the attention and the applause, where we have to make public our every movement, maybe instead we should teach our hearts the difficult task of becoming addicted to the inconspicuous.

Greatness Redefined

I grew up in a church where my pastor was a larger-than-life figure. It's not just that he stood 6'7" tall and spoke with an authority and vocabulary that rivaled anyone, it's that he reached millions of people in his lifetime. It's hard for me to remember a Sunday morning when the altar of our church was not full of people surrendering their hearts to Jesus. He was also responsible for planting thousands of churches in Malawi, Africa, where his crusades would bring tens and hundreds of thousands of people to come and hear the gospel message.

I can vividly remember on numerous occasions him talking about greatness in the kingdom of God. He would explain that although he stood in front of thousands and received much of the attention, he believed there were nursery workers in the back of the church right now, holding a baby, changing an infant, memorizing a verse with a young child, who all would receive greater rewards than him in the kingdom to come. I must admit, each time I heard him utter that phrase I would mutter under my breath, "Yeah, right! What an incredible attempt at humility and what a great way to honor these individuals, but how could a flannel board lesson about

Daniel and the lion's den ever rival an altar full of people giving their hearts to Christ?" How could you begin to compare leading a middle school small group to a packed-out crusade? Much like the disciples in Mark 9 and 10, I failed to understand greatness. I assumed greatness had more to do with the amount of influence one had or the amount of people involved, instead of the act of obedience to what God had called you to do.

I've been blessed to know some truly great people in my lifetime. When I stop to consider who I consider great, it's rarely contingent on the size of their accomplishment and rather on the sacrifice they were willing to make for me and others. Here are some examples. My first-grade teacher, Mrs. Dumbleton, took the time to stop and love a six-year-old boy who had just lost two of his grandfathers and heroes to cancer in six months. Toby, who every year would take a week off work, stay in our dorm at youth camp, and care for a teenage friend of mine with cerebral palsy: changing him, bathing him, pushing his chair through the mud, making sure he got to participate in every event. A friend and intern at my church named Travis, who was willing to come up to the church every morning at 6:00 a.m. so a young man who had recently given his life to Christ could develop a consistent prayer life. Marshall and Cheryl, a couple in their mid 50's, who would spend hours preparing costumes, props, and skits every single week for a Sunday school class of three and four-year-olds. You probably don't know any of these people, but that doesn't mean they aren't the epitome of greatness. I'm sure you could tell your own stories of greatness. The under-the-radar, behind-the-scene heroes who have impacted our lives in such a profound way.

If it's true that not all heroes wear capes, then I believe it's equally true that not all greatness is seen or recognized.

Soul Work

I've sat down with hundreds of people in my office, at a local coffee shop, or at a restaurant for lunch and listened to their stories. They start sharing the details of the circumstances they're currently facing and all the feelings that accompany them. If I've learned anything, it's that every single person has a story of brokenness. Often, the person experiencing this pain will steer the conversation toward questions we've all wrestled with at some point along the way: Why would God do this? How can I move out of this place of suffering and discomfort? What went wrong? Why? Why? Why?

Sometimes I just listen to them. Sometimes I provide a reminder of the character and nature of who God is and what he has promised us in our difficulties. And sometimes, but rarely, an individual will be able to see past what is happening to them and get a glimpse of what God is doing. These times become the deeply enriching moments where real soul work takes place. The place where we don't place our false assumptions and misguided theology upon God, but rather we wrestle with how it's truly possible that, "in all things God works for the good of those who love him, who have been called according to his purpose" (Romans 8:28). That during a situation you can't wait to pass through, something great is giving birth in your soul: dependency and total surrender.

> *The valleys of life or cave moments are where the deepest level of soul work takes place. We are never more open and receptive to being shaped and molded than when we're experiencing the discomfort of the cave. The cave confronts us with the reality of how broken the world is and how we aren't in control like we thought we were. What's important in the cave is that we don't forget the lessons learned in the pasture. Pain, without proper identity in the character of God, will often lead us to disillusionment and confusion. But pain, firmly rooted in the promises of God, can actually become the seed of true growth and transformation.*

David had experienced relative success in almost every area of his life growing up. He was anointed as the next king at a young age, chosen to play the harp for King Saul, defeated Goliath the Philistine giant, and commanded the Israelite armies to success. However, he still ended up sitting in a cave all alone. Every cave experience is difficult, but there is something about that first cave experience that hits the hardest. Especially if you've lived a life where things have just seemed to go your way more often than not. This is why our first cave experience will usually bring about the question: What did I do to get here?

Tim Elmore is the founder of Growing Leaders and has a particular expertise in equipping teachers, leaders, coaches, and parents on how to connect and reach Generations Y and Z. Tim says there are two sets of messages that must be communicated to children as they grow up, one set during childhood and the other set during adolescence. Tim notes that, unfortunately, far too often only one of these sets of messages gets properly communicated, leaving many unprepared.

The first set of messages say this: You are loved. You are unique. You have gifts. You are safe. You are valuable. These messages are imperative to helping a child develop an identity and a foundation that is firm and secure. These messages give them a profound sense of security in which they will grow and gain confidence. It sounds a lot like what we learn in the pasture.

The second set of messages that must be communicated during their adolescence says this: Life is difficult. You are not in control. You are not that important. You are going to die. Your life is not about you. Tim recognizes that this second list may seem harsh, but if an adolescent doesn't come face-to-face with these realities, then he or she will face an adulthood they are unprepared for.[9]

These messages may seem contradictory when you read them, but I believe they are complementary. The pasture roots us in our identity as God's children, but the cave confronts us with the reality of the brokenness around us. Both are essential to God's process. Both are imperative to be the leader God desires. Without one you will eventually be uprooted, and without the other you will be unprepared. A person who knows who they are and whose faith has been tested is moving toward spiritual maturity. A person who is not prepared for the pain and difficulty of life will be thrown off course when the inevitability of brokenness comes their way.

What is it you need to let go of? The future, accomplishing something great, your own plans, the perfect relationship or marriage, the pain of what has happened to you? Maybe the cave is particularly painful because the idols that have so deeply cemented themselves in our lives are now being surgically removed. That's a painful, messy process.

It's hard to compare our stories to Jesus, because we aren't without sin and we can't begin to imagine being the propitiation of sin for all mankind. But even in Jesus's life we see a "letting go" moment. It would have been great if his life could have been years of traveling around the shores of Galilee teaching and healing, but it had to go through Gethsemane. In the garden that evening there was a weight, a burden that seemed to be almost overwhelming. If there was any doubt that Jesus was not only fully divine but also fully human, the garden laid that to rest. Jesus felt the loneliness, the rejection, the weight of what was about to happen.

Jesus uttered simple yet powerful words that revealed everything: "My Father, if it is possible, may this cup be taken from me. Yet not as I will, but as you will" (Matthew 26:39). Jesus spoke like any normal person: "I don't want to experience the pain and suffering of what lies before me." That made his surrender to God all the more notable. This may be the definition of being emptied, of true brokenness, of what it means to "let go." We can join with Jesus as we pray, "God, there is nothing left in me that stands in the way of what you want. There is nothing I haven't or won't lay down if necessary. Every idol that once stood tall in my heart has been torn down. My pride is now submitted to your call. I am fully and totally surrendered." What an incredible place of freedom!

CHAPTER 6

Theology for the Middle

The Waiting Room

Is there anything worse than a waiting room? Currently, all four of my children are under the age of nine. Unfortunately, that makes my wife and I experts in the art of waiting rooms. Two years ago, my son had just had his tonsils and adenoids removed, when a few weeks later he proceeded to fracture his elbow on a trampoline. It took an ER visit, two different surgeries, and a myriad of doctor visits, specialists, and rechecks before he was cleared to resume regular six-year-old activities. Every time we walked into the hospital or doctor's office to a room full of waiting people, my level of anxiety would go up.

Tell me to leave or tell me you can't help, but don't tell me to wait. Especially, in our instant, overnight, express lane, no-wait culture, waiting simply is not an option.

As a result, we believe that time spent waiting is always wasted time. We shouldn't have to ever wait on anything. We should be able to skip ahead and move from preparation to dream, without delay and without obstruction. We know this isn't reality, and yet we live in continual frustration and disillusionment with every moment spent in the in-between.

The Christian walk is all about managing tensions. We manage the tension of being saved by grace and yet allowing our works to be evidence of that transforming grace. We manage the tension of being people of both grace and truth, living under the rule of the kingdom of God while extravagantly loving others. We must also manage the tension of living by radical faith while waiting on God.

Having pastored college students, young professionals, and young families for so many years, I've picked up on the struggle. Every time I preach a message on radical faith, they are ready to quit their job, move to a foreign country, plant a church, or put all the chips on the table. I love this enthusiasm and their willingness to go all in for the gospel. I also know that we are so averse to waiting that we would rather move out on anything than wait for one more minute.

Sometimes radical faith calls us to step off the ledge, and sometimes it calls us to wait. One seems popular and exciting, while the other seems anything but that. I've sat across the table with individuals who felt "called" to leap, but I knew they were struggling with their identity and struggling to remain rooted in their faith. Often, they would use the right spiritual terminology to justify their actions, leaving anything else I had to say as opposition to "what God was leading me to do." Once you have played the "God called me" card, there is very little someone else can speak into the matter. Does God speak to us and guide us? Absolutely. Do we often get the level of clarity we claim to have? Rarely.

I love how Henri Nouwen describes this place in his book *Finding My Way Home*. He talks about how we as believers must practice *active waiting*: a waiting not defined by inactivity but of hope and anticipation.

Most of us consider waiting as something very passive, a hopeless state determined by events totally out of our hands. The bus is late? We cannot do anything about it, so we have to sit there and just wait. It is not difficult to understand the irritation people feel when somebody says, "Just wait." Words like that push us into passivity.

But there is none of this passivity in Scripture. Those who are waiting are waiting very actively. They know that what they are waiting for is growing from the ground on which they are standing. Right here is a secret for us about waiting. If we wait in the conviction that a seed has been planted and that something has already begun, it changes the way we wait. Active waiting implies being fully present to the moment with the conviction that something is happening where we are and that we want to be present to it. A waiting person is someone who is present to the moment, believing that this moment is the moment.[10]

I've never been able to sleep on anything moving, whether it's a car, bus, plane, etc. I will often be on these overnight flights and I'll look around and every single person on the plane is asleep but me. On top of this, my legs get restless if I sit for more than two or three hours. I have to stand up and move around. I'm that guy doing laps around the plane and making everyone uncomfortable and nervous on a ten-hour flight.

> *I've realized there are many Christians who suffer from restless-faith syndrome. They've never developed a "theology for the in-between" or a "theology for the middle." Most of life is not lived in the fulfilment of the calling or on the mountaintop; the majority of life is lived in the in-between moments, in the waiting.*

This "theology for the in-between" is essential to understanding that waiting is not a waste. In fact, the waiting is when God does some of his best work and our level of faith is elevated to the next level. Faith is not always necessary when we're living in the miracle or the fulfillment of the promise, but faith becomes a premium when we can't see the end result.

In his book *A Praying Life,* Paul Miller writes, "When you persist in a spiritual vacuum, when you hang in there during ambiguity, you get to know God."[11] The waiting, that is, the essence of faith, provides the context for relationship. In fact, the only way intimacy grows in any relationship is through persisting through the difficulty and unknown.

David became a professional at waiting. Most are willing to wait several months, at the most a few years, but not ten to fifteen years. There is no way that God's call would be drawn out over such a long length of time. In fact, if God is in it, then we should expect to see results as soon as we submit to walk in obedience, right? We're willing to submit to God's call, as long as the waiting fits our approved standard of length.

Waiting is usually viewed as an unnecessary waste. Our technological advancements and at-your-fingertips capabilities have led us to believe that we can easily bypass the process and arrive at our destination. In a moment our video can go viral, our company take off, or our music become mainstream. What used to take weeks, months, or years can now take moments.

We've essentially eliminated waiting. We have call-ahead seating, instant messaging, pre-check lines, apps to avoid traffic, online check-in, and grocery shopping pickup or delivery. Many of these advancements have added incredible value to my life and simultaneously led me to believe that I should never have to wait ever again. Anything that is not instant and immediate creates frustration.

As a result, we jump on social media and see our friends, acquaintances, and total strangers living out their dreams, making a difference, having their perfect families, or venturing into entrepreneurial endeavors, and we start to get restless. We begin looking around at our less-than-sexy nine to five job, our twelve-year-old Honda Accord, and our recent vacation to Kansas City with the family, and we feel the pull to make something happen. This is not a book intended to stifle the entrepreneurial spirit God has placed in so many of us. Rather, it is intended to allow us to see what is primary: what is bigger than our endeavors or achievements, and what God may be trying to do inside us. We cannot simply bypass every season of waiting simply because it's uncomfortable. Most of us are so good at removing or avoiding anything in our life that is uncomfortable, and, as a result, we remove the very thing we need the most. It's often in the middle of our discomfort where God is moving and stirring and shaping us the most.

Eugene Peterson says it like this: "Another will is greater, wiser and more intelligent than my own. So I wait. Waiting means that there is Another whom I trust and from whom I receive. My will, important and essential as it is, finds a Will that is more important, more essential... In prayer we are aware that God is in action and that when the circumstances are ready, when others are in the right place and when my heart is prepared, I will be called into action. Waiting in prayer is a disciplined refusal to act before God acts. Waiting is our participation in the process that results in the 'time fulfilled.'"[12]

For the past several years I've traveled around the world helping train church planters. For many, this involves taking them through a process of evaluation, assessment, training, coaching, and launching. Having done these enough times, I've picked up on tendencies that are relatively consistent. One of these tendencies is that most church planters are willing to shortcut the pre-launch phase of fundraising, training, and planning in order to launch their weekly worship gathering. There is an allure that if they can just start meeting, then it will grow and begin to build itself. I often have to help them rewire their understanding. Churches who are willing to embrace the pre-launch process of preparation are exponentially healthier than those who just want to "get it off the ground.

In fact, it is often these church planters who have shortcut the process that come back to me just a few months or years into their journey and realize their need for further training and preparation. They should have embraced the slow process of gestation instead of giving birth to something that was premature.

I find it interesting that throughout the Bible we see the period of waiting becomes the very context where faith is actualized. It's the place where our faith is truly tested. I think it's easy, especially if you grew up hearing the stories of the Bible, to simply read over certain stories and assume that it was easier for the characters in the Bible to believe God than it is for you. We can think that somehow Noah, Moses, Jacob, Joseph, and Esther possessed a special call from God that made their faith a certainty. It's easy to have faith when we have the luxury of reading the complete story from beginning to end. In hindsight, we can look back and see where God intervened and how he was in control of the entire situation. But what about when we don't have the benefit of hindsight? What about when we're in the midst of our waiting season? Do we really believe that the same God who began a work in our lives will complete the task?

What about when you're way, *way* past the possibility of having children, and God promised that your descendants would be as numerous as the stars in the sky? Would Abraham and Sarah believe? When you've received a vision that God would use you in a position of authority and influence, but you've been abandoned, forgotten, wrongly accused, and are spending the prime years of your life in a prison? Would Joseph hold onto the vision he received from God? You've entered into an agreement to serve seven years for the hand of Rachel in marriage, but instead you're deceived and it takes you fourteen years. Would Jacob be willing to wait? You've received a special calling to lead God's people to their destination, but instead you spend forty years wandering around in the worst possible conditions. Would Moses trust God in the wilderness journey? Your people are in danger of being massacred and your entrance to the king could cost you your life? Would Esther be willing to trust God knowing the potential outcome? In every scenario the main character had reason to doubt. They could have gone the other direction, given up on what God had spoken, or chosen to abandon the call. They could have falsely assumed about God that waiting always equals lack of involvement.

I find it rather amazing that when I look back, I can clearly see God's hand leading me through every stage of my life. Foresight, on the other hand, the unknown that lies before us, will often breed fear. What has actually happened produces faith, while what may or may not happen produces fear. We think we need more and more foresight, when really what we need is to continue to stay rooted in what God has always done, his continued faithfulness through every step of our lives.

The waiting is one of the key places in life that makes the fulfillment of God's promises so incredible. It's where we've learned to struggle, be refined, let go, and ultimately trust God no matter the situation. What happens in the waiting is that there are moments that simply don't seem like the destination will ever arrive. We begin trusting in who God is and not what he can do for us. And it's in these moments of testing where our fragile understanding of God begins to solidify. That's why the waiting season is so essential to our lives. Without it, we would begin to put our faith in what we see instead of the promises that so often go unseen.

Let's play the what-if game for a minute! What if Joseph had gone from living with his family in the land of Israel to an overnight success story?

Would he have trusted God with all his heart? Would he have the character and integrity to lead as a godly leader? Would he eventually abandon his sole commitment to Yahweh for the gods of Egypt? When we read the setbacks in the life of Joseph, we see how God was orchestrating and using every step to lead Joseph to the place God had called him. Why don't we understand our setbacks and seasons of waiting in the same light? Because we don't believe God has a plan for our lives like he did for Joseph? Because Joseph was somehow more special than us or had a unique calling? Because we think our mistakes have somehow disqualified us from his plan? Because we simply don't have the faith to believe that there is a purpose in our waiting?

Think about these waiting seasons from a very practical position. Without waiting, without learning to persevere and trust and hold onto hope, we would never be able to navigate the inevitable setbacks and challenges of life. We would fold under the pressure or assume that we had missed God along the way.

The book of Hebrews tells us that every single one of us is in a waiting season as long as we are on this earth. Even these heroes of the faith didn't see the complete fulfillment of what they were waiting for. "All these people were still living by faith when they died. They did not receive the things promised; they only saw them and welcomed them from a distance, admitting that they were foreigners and strangers on earth" (Hebrews 11:13).

As followers of Jesus we are living as foreigners and strangers in a place that is not our home. As long as we are living in this tent of a body, separated from eternity in his presence, we are waiting. We are living by faith in what we know we will never fully experience in this life.

The Dips

The planning fallacy is a theory, first proposed by Daniel Kahneman and Amos Tversky in 1979, which makes predictions about how much time will be needed to complete a future task. This phenomenon states that when an individual predicts a time, they usually display two common characteristics: an optimistic bias and an underestimation of the time needed.[13]

They go on to conclude that we still have the tendency to be optimistic about the time needed to complete something, even if past history shows otherwise. It's also incredibly interesting to note that individuals are exceedingly optimistic when predicting the time needed for their own tasks, but pessimistic when predicting the tasks of others. In other words, it will usually always take longer than you planned or desired.

Think of life like you think of any sort of construction project. Whether you're building a new home or a business, you might as well double the amount of money and time you think it's going to take. This is why you must develop a "theology for the middle," because you are going to spend the majority of your life in transition or in-between. There will be unforeseen circumstances, delays, and situations you cannot plan for. There will be cave moments when, just like David, you will slow down, look around, and try to make sense of what just transpired.

Along with the planning fallacy, I believe many of us hold to a linear trajectory fallacy: a common belief that as long as we do the right things, our life will continually be progressing up and to the right, continually improving as we go. But life doesn't take us continually up and to the right. If anything, life is a series of S--curves where we experience mountaintops followed by dips, inevitable obstacles that take us from the mountaintop into a new valley. These dips don't take us back to square one, but instead they reposition us to a place where we must learn a new strategy in order to continue moving forward. This becomes a cycle of growth and development in our lives.

The dips, or the bottom of the curve, become a place where we learn, reposition, pivot our strategy, and make the necessary changes in order to move forward. Ask the owner or CEO of any growing company or organization, and they will tell you that without the dips they would have never made the necessary changes that would ultimately propel them forward into the next phase of growth. These dips can do the same for us if we allow them.

The Disillusionment

Ryan gave his heart to Christ at sixteen years old and never looked back. It wasn't just a casual decision made after an emotional sermon, but a complete surrender of his life. Everyone who knew Ryan could immediately see the transformation that had taken place in him in just a very short time. He got connected in the church, regularly attended a Bible study, and was being discipled by an older mentor. At one point, Ryan began to think that eventually he would become a pastor or missionary and help lead others into this new life he had found in Christ.

Upon graduation, Ryan decided to attend a small Bible college about three hours from his hometown. He moved into the dorms, established his first semester schedule, and was excited about the possibilities for growth that awaited him.

It didn't take long before the excitement of what was possible was traded for the disappointment of his new reality. He imagined an environment where the majority of the student body were growing in discipleship and engaged in deepening spiritual formation practices. Instead, he discovered that many of those who raised their hands in worship during chapel were also engaged in an array of morally questionable activities or downright hypocrisy throughout the week. The Bible classes he assumed would deepen and enlighten his understanding of truth, instead were led by professors who were causing him to question and even doubt many of the foundational truths of his faith. The church near campus that many of the students attended was still reeling from the moral failure of the previous pastor, and there was widespread disagreement about who should be the next pastor.

Disillusionment is defined as a feeling of disappointment resulting from the discovery that something is not as good as one believed it to be. With the Christian faith, comes moments and seasons of disillusionment. This feeling is often brought about when what we know about God and what we see in our lives don't align. It also happens when what we see in other Christians and what we see in the church don't align with what we believed about them. It's in these moments where we come to a fork in the road. Do we go left because we find it impossible to reconcile the hypocrisy that exists all around us, or do we go right and lean into our faith and seek to find something that is genuine and authentic?

Let me make this guarantee: We will have opportunities around every corner to walk the path of cynicism. People will fail us. Christians will sell their souls to a political affiliation. Leaders and pastors will say one thing and do another. The church will be less than what they should be at times. We will be betrayed, offended, and let down. Some dreams will die. The person we admire more than anyone in the world will prove to be broken and capable of sin. And in every one of these moments, we will have a choice.

Don't be deceived. Don't take the bait. It may seem like cynicism is the only way, but it is the cowardly way. It will destroy our souls and rob us of the beauty of life, love, and grace.

> *With life, with pain, and with disappointment comes the temptation to allow our hearts to become hard. To close off. To keep people at arm's length. To become a cynic. And there might not be anything in the world as tragic as a cynic. Cynicism can be seen as a defense mechanism to protect us from disappointment, but the tradeoff is that we never truly live. To me, cynicism is the result of those who have let go of hope and stopped seeing the beauty, grace, and goodness that is all around.*

As a cynic, we become numb to the world around us and assume that every person has an angle. We miss the beauty in life because all we can see is the destruction or the hypocrisy. We can't experience the joy of genuine friendships, because we're too busy looking over our shoulder or trying to find their misstep or angle. We can't see the splendor of God's redemptive work, because all we see is the mess or how we were wronged.

Paul Miller talks about how a life of prayer and a life of cynicism are antithetical in almost every way. "To be cynical is to be distant. While offering a false intimacy of being 'in the know,' cynicism actually destroys intimacy. It leads to a creeping bitterness that can deaden and even destroy the spirit."[14] Prayer kills a heart of cynicism, because it removes us from the throne of our hearts and replaces it with a heart of flesh.

I remember reading C.S. Lewis's *Screwtape Letters* as a young theology student pursuing my undergraduate degree. It was enlightening and opened my eyes to see the ways in which our adversary, Satan, strategizes for our destruction. Seeds are planted years earlier in your life, which can eventually sprout into beautiful flowers or destructive weeds. Good things can move into idolatry. A lack of identity can flow into addiction.

There was one part of the book that seemed to jump off the page at me. Screwtape and his nephew Wormwood are demons and are attempting to destroy a young man, known in the book as the Patient. Their goal is that the Patient will spend eternity in hell. They have thrown the proverbial kitchen sink at this young man, and yet he seems to stay resolved in his faith. They have tried fear, the negative influence of friends, sexual pleasure, and more. At one point, Wormwood, the young nephew in training, seems to think they have lost all hope for bringing the young man down. Screwtape, however, believes that there are several tactics still at their disposal to bring the young man to destruction and ruin. In fact, the Patient has become quite the church shopper, jumping from place to place and subtly critiquing what is right and wrong about each place he visits.

Screwtape writes to Wormwood saying, "The search for a 'suitable' church makes the man a critic where God wants him to be a pupil."[15] And if we can make him a critic where God wants him to be a pupil, then it is only a matter of time until that road leads to the inevitable destination of disillusionment, cynicism, and mistrust.

The enemy deceives the believer into thinking that just because they are avoiding the "major" sins and temptations of those who are truly "lost," they are justified in becoming a critic. And what happens is that slowly, over time, we move from disciples at the feet of Jesus to the Pharisees and teachers of the law. The inside of the cup grows increasingly dirty while we spend more and more time making sure the outside of our cup, and the outside of your cup, is pristine. And here's the scariest part about this transition. Often pride has blinded us from even being able to see it. We can be living the very definition of a Pharisee but be so deceived into believing we are the true disciples sitting at the feet of Jesus. We have become the older brother in the story who stands outside the feast wondering why his father would ever throw a feast for his prodigal brother who just returned home.

You know what is amazing about cynicism? That two people can have the exact same experiences and see the exact same things and have two completely opposing takeaways. That the heart of the cynic and the heart of a loving father or mother are not determined by what *has* happened or what *is* happening, but by what they choose to see.

CHAPTER 7

Scars

Wounded Healers

If you live life, you will have scars. If a group of us were sitting together at dinner, we could go around the table and tell stories about the various scars we have on our bodies. The scars are a constant reminder of what happened, so it's almost impossible to forget. I bet some of your scars have some really great stories.

I've got a long scar on my shin. I was playing capture the flag in the prayer gardens at the Christian university I attended, when I attempted to jump from the upper level down to the garden below, about a twelve-foot drop. I was successful on the jump and landing, but since it was nearly midnight I couldn't see the landscape edging right in front of me. I was running full speed, so, when I tripped, my shin went into the edging about two to three centimeters and then scraped forward about two to three inches. It's a good one.

I've got a scar on the top of my head from hitting an air conditioning unit in the basement of a soup kitchen in Harlem, New York. I didn't realize I had hit my head so hard, and when I came up out of the basement I had blood pouring from the side of the chef's hat I was wearing. To say the least, I scared everyone eating that day.

My wife has a ten-inch scar down the middle of her stomach where she had emergency surgery to remove a diseased kidney when she was two years old.

All our scars tell a story. I've learned that physical scars are actually much easier to overcome than emotional or spiritual scars. Every physical scar becomes like a badge of honor, but emotional and spiritual scars can become wounds that never really heal.

Scars can become a reminder of God's grace that point us to his coming redemption, or they can actually keep us from becoming fully surrendered, trapping us in the past.

As a pastor, almost weekly I get the chance to sit down and hear someone's story. You would think by this time nothing would shock me, but that just isn't true. I still can't believe some of the predicaments and situations that we all find ourselves in at times. I can't believe the level of brokenness so many people must endure.

Not long ago I sat down with a clean-cut, well-articulated, twenty-five-year-old male who looked like he had it all together. His story included being sexually molested by numerous male family members growing up, which forced him to leave home at an early age.

The next several years he simply tried to survive while experimenting with everything from alcohol to prescription drugs to methamphetamines. I sat across the table mesmerized that this young man had experienced so much in his life at such a young age. While I was trying to make the eighth-grade baseball team, he was on his own, making a living by finding and selling whatever he could get his hands on.

Give me 1,000 attempts, and I never would have guessed his story. Needless to say, his story has and will forever shape him. Your story might not be that dramatic, but you've got a story that shapes who you are today. In my experience, I've found that your story either propels you into the life God has called you to live, or it is continually grasping at your heels in an attempt to hold you back. It either becomes a launching pad and motivating factor to achieve something better, or it can easily become like a boulder tied around your waist.

The young man who sat before me had every right to be angry, bitter, and leery of anyone who attempted to gain his trust. Instead, this young man exuded the characteristics of confidence and approachability. I couldn't help but ask questions concerning how he overcame such incredible obstacles.

I'm not a counselor or psychiatrist and wouldn't begin to delve into the healing process of someone who has experienced something as devastating as child molestation. It's something many of us couldn't begin to wrap our minds around. Here's what I do know. Every day I see these people, the wounded healers, walking around our church, working on our staff, and heading off to their jobs. They're wounded because the pain is real, the process has been difficult, and the memories won't ever go away. This process of healing often takes a considerable amount of time and can require months or years to fully process. They're healers because they've chosen to use their stories to bring healing to those going through similar situations. The hope they have in Christ's coming and the redemption of all things that have been broken is greater than the pain of what they've had to endure.

There is something amazing, I would even say supernatural, that occurs when someone chooses to take their pain, their scars, and use them to bring healing to others. When they get past themselves, process the pain, and begin helping others in the process of healing and recovery, they actually begin receiving the healing. We are healed and increasingly made whole when we provide healing. As Macrina Diederkehr says in her book *Seasons of the Heart*, "I'm learning to befriend my scars and find the gifts hidden underneath."[16]

I've watched as people have shared their story of how their child died at age three, how they battled with an eating disorder until they were thirty-five, how their spouse cheated on them with their best friend, or how they've been fighting a disease for the last fifteen years. As they talk, you can sense the struggle and see the pain they've had to endure walking through these seasons of life. I've also watched as these people have embraced the pain, pointed to their scars, and now use their story to bring hope to others. The scars are like a huge neon arrow pointing to the day when God will make ALL things new.

Is there anything that brings more glory to God and disarms the plans of the enemy than allowing God to take our pain and brokenness and using it as a picture of God's redemption? Men and women, who in the very midst of their deep wounding, sense the presence and peace of God all around them. When we take what was meant for destruction and ruin and it becomes living proof that God takes dead things, resurrects them, and gives them life again. It's proof that nothing is beyond his grasp or out of his reach or worthy of being thrown away.

Your story may not be overly dramatic, but I bet it's filled with up and downs, highs and lows, obstacles and pain. When I look through scripture, I'm encouraged to see that pain was usually a prerequisite for God to use someone. It was a result of the scars, the pain, the suffering, that God was able to use humble men and women to do the work of the kingdom of God. There's something about suffering that positions us to be used by God.

James 1:2-4 says: "Consider it pure joy, my brothers, whenever you face trials of many kinds, because you know that the testing of your faith develops perseverance. Perseverance must finish its work so that you may be mature and complete, not lacking anything."

This is one of those paradoxes of the kingdom of God. It just doesn't make sense, and it's definitely not natural to rejoice when we face trials. At least not for me. These trials, however, may just be the very thing God is using to prepare us for what's ahead. It may be the very thing that is positioning us to be used by God.

We've all been wounded. Each and every one of us walks around with scars; some scars are bigger than others. Each and every one of us also has a choice to make. Do we walk around and use the scars as a crutch, or do we point to the scars and tell the story of healing? Do we use our scars to bring hope to people who are still hurting? In the end, we've all been wounded, the question is whether we will use the scars to tell a story of hope. I believe our world needs wounded healers more than ever before. Men and women who walk in brokenness and humility and yet the freedom and resurrection that only comes through Christ in us. People who are willing to admit the pain is real, the questions are many, and the threads of despair sometimes linger, and yet the God of resurrection and redemption is still at work.

The Gaps

I had only heard stories about my eighth-grade algebra teacher, Mr. Reisner. I had passed him in the hall on occasion, and I was already fearful about what to expect. The stories, told over and over again by a bunch of middle schoolers, had portrayed him to be the devil incarnate. On top of this, I had always struggled with math and was already preparing for the longest school year imaginable. I remember sitting in the first class and waiting to experience what everyone had described. And then the second class and the third class, and so on. I'm not going to sit here and tell you that Mr. Reisner was Mary Poppins, but he was far from what I had been led to believe or what I had been concocting in my head.

I've learned in my life that I have a tendency to fill in the gaps. When I only get a little bit of information or when there is an unknown, I can easily assume the worst or begin believing something rather far from the truth. I can do this with circumstances, with people, and even with my relationship with God. We all have a tendency to do this when we're dealing with the unknown. As people living under God's kingdom rule, we are directed to take control of our minds and align our thinking with the truth of God's Word. These truths become a guiding and steadying force when it may be rather easy to allow our minds to fill in the gaps or fabricate our own understanding.

There can be a tendency to do this during moments of suffering when our understanding of God is often being informed by what is happening around us or what we see. This is when faith gets tested. Faith is trusting in the truth of who God is, especially when there are visible opportunities to question this truth or no evidence to back up our faith claims.

Any confusion concerning the nature or character of God will usually surface when you're in the cave. Nothing will ever cause you to question the goodness of God, his sovereignty, or his justice more than suffering. Suffering has this way of making us believe things about God's character and nature that are simply untrue. It's in these moments that any house built on something other than the hope of Jesus Christ begins to crack and we're forced to try to make sense of what is happening around us. If there are looming doubts about God's goodness or if someone hasn't properly processed the implications of living in a world of competing kingdoms, the cave brings these issues front and center.

I think that one of the major factors that trips people up more than anything is reconciling a good God with their suffering. If God truly is sovereign and all-sufficient, then how can he allow this suffering to take place in my life? How can I reconcile a God who loves me and a God who would allow _____ to happen?

YouVersion, the Bible app, reports that in the United States in 2017 the most popular verse was Romans 8:28: "And we know that in all things, God works for the good of those who love Him, who have been called according to His purpose."[17] This doesn't surprise me at all, because we are all searching for a way to make sense of our pain and to give others a context for their pain and suffering. We want to believe the words of Romans 8:28 that ALL things are truly working out for our good, whether we recognize it or not.

It's not that the Bible has been silent about suffering, it's that often our theology and understanding of life has not truly been shaped by scripture. Let's use 1 Peter as an example. We know the Christians to whom Peter was writing were engaged in a changing culture that was becoming increasingly hostile to the Christian faith. Right from the beginning of the book, Peter reminds them of something that must constantly be at the forefront of their believing, thinking, and living.

"Peter, an apostle of Jesus Christ, To God's elect, exiles scattered throughout the provinces of Pontus, Galatia, Cappadocia, Asia and Bithynia, who have been chosen according to the foreknowledge of God the Father." (1 Peter 1:1-2)

First, you are God's elect. You, through your faith in Jesus Christ, have become one of God's special people. Secondly, you're EXILES! You are currently occupying a place that is not your home. Remember, you were designed and created for intimate communion with the Father (Genesis 1-2), but it was sin that separated us from that intimacy with our heavenly Father (Genesis 3). God's story is a story of redemption, of reclaiming his people for intimate relationship with him once again.

In suffering, we begin to lose our footing in the bigger narrative of God's redemptive story. We lose sight of the fall and the devastating effects of sin and death on creation. We stop rooting ourselves in a story that is about our redemption and God reclaiming relationship with us, which had been severed in the Garden of Eden. We forget that we are still operating in a world of competing kingdoms where light and darkness exists and justice does not always prevail. Suffering often causes us to let go of the rope and lose sight that, even in the midst of devastation, this is still a love story and the end of the movie has already been determined.

But here's what we must remember. We are currently situated between the first and second coming, between the already and the not-yet. In a world of competing kingdoms, it's our job to spread the rule of God's kingdom in our lives and wherever we go. This also means the reality of the kingdom of darkness: where destruction, suffering, pain, disasters, and disease also exists. You and I won't live forever. Right now, our bodies are currently in a process of decay.

This provides us a context for suffering and the character of God. If we recognize that we are exiles, strangers, and aliens in a world that is not our home, then we will prepare ourselves for the suffering that will happen as long as we are occupants of this world. As followers of Jesus, we should not be shocked at the trials and suffering we will face. The Bible is not shy about this, but, on numerous points throughout the New Testament, it prepares us for how to respond.

In 1 Peter, he goes from reminding the church they are exiles to teaching them how to stand in a challenging culture. Toward the end of the book he develops a theme of suffering leading to grace, which anchors us in hope. Although we will experience the suffering of living in a world of competing kingdoms, God's grace will empower us to endure and to stand firm, knowing that the anchor for our souls is the hope of salvation, the hope of eternity. In essence, Peter does not tie them to the hope of their situation or even their deliverance from suffering, something he could not guarantee. He anchors them in the only sure thing, the only thing he can guarantee will not fail.

Could it be that too often our lives are only tied to the answer to a prayer or the deliverance from our situation? If God delivers, then we will trust him. If God answers our cries of desperation, then he must be good. Or can we believe that he is 100 percent good and completely in control, even if that means holding onto the anchor of eternity with him? What if we tied ourselves to something that was unchanging and immovable? Let's tie ourselves to his goodness and the hope of eternity, for everything else will lead us astray.

Ditches

On your journey of faith, you will soon realize how easy it is to fall into a ditch. Every single one of us will wrestle with this at some point. A ditch is an overcompensation of a belief you now hold because of something you've experienced or something you've believed. Theological ditches are caused by something we've experienced or by an overcorrection concerning something we've believed.

For example, if you grew up around people who only talked about works and holiness, maybe you decide you will only talk about love and grace. Or if you were a part of a church where the leadership or pastor deeply hurt you, then you choose to practice faith apart from the church or any hierarchy of leadership. Maybe you're reading your Bible one day, and there is a whole section you can't justify or defend, so, as a result, the Bible becomes more of a guide to life than a source of authority.

There are ditches everywhere! If we look deep within ourselves, we can probably identify a few. All of them point back to something I experienced or believed. I have to fight the tendency to take something I'm passionate about and overcorrect or extend beyond the necessary boundaries of what is balanced, healthy, and orthodox.

One of the issues I often see people wrestling with are the concepts of blessing and suffering. There is a whole thread of belief circulating in churches where God is just here to bless you, and if you aren't experiencing blessing, then something is deficient in your faith. This way of believing leaves people abandoned and alone when they're walking through their Cave of Adullum. This is one ditch.

Others have responded to this bless-me theology by developing their own sadistic theology where the depth of your faith is derived from the amount of suffering you're willing to endure. Because suffering is a reality of genuine faith, they begin to view suffering as a badge to be worn, so if you're not suffering then you're not really living a genuine faith. Here is another ditch.

Many evangelical Christians in America have placed an emphasis on a profession of faith and belief in Christ, without aligning their morals, politics, and way of life around the gospel and kingdom living. As a result, a growing number of Christians have abandoned traditional evangelical beliefs for a social gospel, in which the emphasis is on reaching the poor and marginalized and bringing justice to oppressive structures. Both are absolutely necessary but, when separated from each other, become ditches. Instead of choosing one or the other, we must find a place where true repentance and confession leads us to reorient our lives around the gospel, a life on mission, and a love for the marginalized and oppressed – a holistic gospel.

Ditches are easy to fall into because we're human beings with feelings, experiences, and a natural propensity to want to correct someone we believe is wrong. Unfortunately, often when we identify a ditch we overcorrect and, as a result, find ourselves in a ditch on the opposite side of the road.

Let's root this discussion in the greater story of God. To understand this, you have to understand the implications of the kingdom of God. The kingdom of God is what Jesus talked about more than anything else, and yet I can probably count on one hand how many sermons I've heard preached on this topic in my lifetime. The majority of Christians are wildly deficient in our understanding of God's kingdom.

The Garden of Eden was a place where God's kingdom experienced complete, unhindered rule. God got what God wanted, and what he wanted was communion with his creation, especially Adam and Eve, who, unlike the rest of creation, were formed in his image. In Genesis 3, a new dynamic now comes on the scene. Sin and death now enter the equation and the unhindered rule of God is now interrupted. A separation now exists between God and his creation. What takes place next is an existence where two kingdoms are at work—two kingdoms that are diametrically opposed to each other in every way.

> *And it is this reality of living between the tension of two competing kingdoms that cause many of our greatest struggles to belief. We are forced wrestle with the implications of sin, decay, and death while simultaneously living in the reality of God's kingdom drawing near through the work of Jesus. The cave forces us to sit in this tension.*

We know from scripture that from Genesis 3 to the present day the goal has been redemption of God's people and to reinstitute a new heaven and a new earth, a place where once again God's kingdom will reign without hindrance. Through Jesus we now have access to the realities of the kingdom of heaven. Because of the work done through the cross and resurrection, we can take part right now in the blessings that come along with being God's redeemed people. However, many of the blessings and promises afforded us in God's kingdom will come to their fruition when God will once again reign in completion, when the kingdom of darkness has been completely eliminated. Right now, we still live in a world where we can live in the realities of the kingdom of heaven while we are still affected by the existence of the kingdom of darkness. This means that bad things still happen to God's people, disease exists, natural disasters rain down on the moral and immoral, death is an inevitability, and justice doesn't always prevail.

This tension has created the impasse that so many Christians struggle to cross. We expect our lives to be free of suffering and problems, almost as if we expect our current reality to reflect our future reality of eternity with Christ. Because God is both sovereign over all of creation and all-powerful, if suffering happens it is only because God is permitting it. How can a good God allow innocent people to become victims? Herein lies the portion of our theological understanding that often needs to be reworked. We falsely assume that the blessings of being "in Christ" give us a free pass. This is not to say that God's hand doesn't rest on his people or that he doesn't deliver us from situations. It confirms, however, that we are not beyond the reach of suffering in this world. Suffering does not for one instance deny God's involvement.

If you want to know what the blessings are that we get to experience when joining the work of Christ, I urge you to open your Bible and begin reading the Sermon on the Mount (Matthew 5-7). You'll soon realize the blessed life has very little to do with external things or possessions or situations and everything to do with the joy and life and hope we have by being people of the kingdom of God. God is calling the marginalized and destitute to gather around him and is showing them that no matter their socioeconomic status or past failures, they can consider themselves blessed because of the availability of God's kingdom.

We can't forget this when we're experiencing our cave moments. We might not consider ourselves blessed when we're walking through whatever sadness or darkness or pain that we're enduring, but remember that's exactly who Jesus was saying was "blessed" in the Beatitudes. Blessed are you who are "poor in Spirit" or those who "mourn" or the "persecuted" or the "reviled," for the kingdom of God is open and available for you to enter (Matthew 5:1-11). We are blessed because the realities of the kingdom of God that lead to life and eternity are forever ours, and nobody and nothing can take that away.

The word "blessed" used in Matthew 5 and Luke 6 is *makarios*, which refers to the highest type of well-being possible for human beings. We often use the term "blessed" to refer to something external we've received—a new job, great children, a raise at work—, but when you understand *makarios*, you realize that being "blessed" is a reality of God's kingdom both now and forever, not what you may or may not be receiving personally or in the moment.

In the cave, don't blame God, even though you may find it easy to do. Don't fall into the ditch of believing your pain is from your heavenly Father, when the story of God is about your redemption; it's about him restoring his relationship with us so that one day we can once again fully live in his kingdom, the place where God gets what God wants: UNHINDERED RELATIONSHIP WITH YOU!

CHAPTER 8

Clarity Addicts

Fork in the Road

Meet Lacey. She's twenty-six years old and currently working as a project assistant at a digital advertising agency in the downtown area. She has a degree in social work, and for the past four years she's been looking for opportunities to work with underprivileged families and youth in an impoverished area of her city. She's currently serving with a local program that provides mentors for at-risk youth about to age out of the foster care system. A friend of hers just told her about a new opportunity in another city where they're hiring individuals to move into strategic areas of the city to identify and create transformational programs working with local children. Lacey decides to apply and receives a phone call about a week later. Although they can't hire her right now, if she's willing to move and work alongside them as a volunteer, it will increase her chance of being hired in the future.

What does Lacey do? She has prayed about it but hasn't necessarily received an answer. Does she quit her job (and paycheck), uproot from her network of friends and family, and pursue an opportunity that may or may not work out? She seeks counsel from a lifelong friend, from one of the pastors at her local church, and from a coworker she respects. She's looking for anything: a sign, an open door, a closed door, a word of wisdom, anything. She wonders whether this will work out. What if she goes, and it turns into an absolute disaster? What if she moves, and it's not God's will at all? There seems to be a lot that is hanging in the balance.

I've learned that one of our greatest fears is the fear of missing God's will. You come to a fork in the road and assume that one direction leads to the blessed life, a life where your dreams will come true, and the other direction leads to failure: God removing his hand from you altogether. As a result, you are paralyzed by the fear of getting it wrong.

But what about those moments when we're unsure? When God hasn't spoken or written our answer on the wall? This is when it gets a little trickier. This is when our own selfish motives and desires can easily get thrown into the mix and confused for God's direction. I don't believe we are to walk around in fear that we are going to miss God's will. I think his grace is sufficient for us and that as we seek him, he leads us. The unknown can either fuel our fear of the future or fuel our trust in God. We get to choose.

Honestly, this entire book could be about navigating the will of God. There are principles throughout scripture we can apply. There are things we can deduct from the character and nature of God. There are also things that are a mystery; things unknown apart from a personal relationship of intimacy with Christ and the indwelling power of the Holy Spirit in us. I do believe God still speaks, and when we reject his leading we are walking in disobedience. I also believe the path is clear when we're talking about issues that will lead us away from our relationship with Christ. But what about a circumstance where we really need to know which way to go? Do I take that job? Do I go to that school? Do I move to that city? Marry that person? Start that business? These decisions paralyze us. They imprison us in a fear of getting it wrong. There is so much at stake, that we must have certainty for such a big decision.

> *I believe one of the reasons we fear missing God's will is because we lack a personal, intimate relationship with our heavenly Father. A God we worship at a distance will always create more fear than trust. A person who knows their Father is good and loving and wants the best for them doesn't live in constant fear. A person who sees God as ambivalent and demanding will*

always live in fear of making the wrong choice. So maybe we should start with this question: how do we see our heavenly Father?

Here are some good questions that help guide us into understanding God's will. Have we spent time in solitude listening? Moments where we embrace the silence and don't speak, but remain in a posture of listening. Have we fasted and prayed about the situation? Fasting can bring our flesh into submission and open us to see what the Spirit may want to speak to our situation. Have we sought counsel from wise, godly individuals and people of authority in our life? God often speaks through channels of authority. Have we submitted our life, our situation, and our future to God? Will the decisions we're about to make draw us closer to Christ or farther away from him? Are our motives pure and does it honor God? I don't believe God always gives us door A and B so that we must determine which one leads to blessing and which one leads to destruction. I believe God looks at something bigger than the decision right in front of us; he looks at our heart, our motives, and our desires. As we surrender ourselves, our will becomes more equally aligned with him and his plan for our lives.

Throughout scripture, we see God speaking to individuals in supernatural ways. But more often we see men and women who have surrendered their lives to Christ and are open to the leading of the Holy Spirit. They don't receive a vision, a prophetic word, or handwriting on a wall, and yet they trust that God is not only involved but guiding their every step. They lived without perfect clarity but with a fully surrendered life.

This is the most difficult part of discovering God's will: it's rarely revealed to us beforehand and is something we experience as we walk out a life of faith and surrender. As Jesus taught his disciples to pray, "Father, your kingdom come, your will be done, on earth as it is in heaven." It sounds rather basic but the ramifications of such a prayer are profound. God, I willingly choose to lay down my wants, my desires, and my plans for your will. I willingly submit myself to your process, whatever the circumstances may be. I let go of the rope of my future because I am limited and finite in my knowledge and understanding. Again, it's not denying that God speaks and leads and directs, but isn't his will for our lives that we learn to live by faith? Isn't it faith that he ultimately desires? That we become accustomed to the unknown, the uncertainty, and the risk; learning to "trust the Lord with all our hearts and not lean on our own understanding" (Proverbs 3:5).

Every time you take a step of faith, you are practicing the discipline of self-denial and choosing to believe that God is ultimately in control of all things. You are choosing to live and walk and act by faith; something God desires for each of us. "And without faith it is impossible to please God, because anyone who comes to him must believe that he exists and that he rewards those who earnestly seek him" (Hebrews 11:6). Somehow, in our current culture, we've become full-blown, outright clarity addicts. We see living by faith as knowing what to do instead of stepping into the unknown and fully trusting his sovereignty.

So maybe the question is not do I go left or right at the fork in the road? Maybe the bigger question is whether my will, my plans, my dreams, and my heart are fully surrendered to him. Do I desire his will to be accomplished in me, or am I living for my own agenda? There might not be any prayer more difficult to pray than, "Father, your will be done." In that moment you are completely relinquishing any control you thought you had. You are letting go of the reins and putting your trust in something higher, something greater.

Think on stories you've learned from scripture. How often does God honor the lives of those individuals who are fully surrendered to him? How often does he move in the lives of those who are fully trusting in him? Although learning to discern the voice of God and the leading of the Holy Spirit is crucial, we also see men and women of God throughout the scriptures who aren't stepping out with a clear direction, but instead with a desire to see the kingdom of God expand and the mission of God go forth.

Our culture is obsessed with knowing, and as a result we are living in fear of getting it wrong. What if we were equally obsessed with submitting our whole lives to him? Laying down our idols and walking in complete submission and obedience?

It seems like I have daily conversations with individuals who are just about to graduate from college or grad school or are in a major career transition and want to know what's next. The entire dilemma is rooted in several things that are constantly fueling our fears: the unknown or possibly missing our opportunity. We have difficulty learning to embrace a process that is not clearly laid out in front of us. We want to know! We want answers! We want to eliminate the need for questions, and, as a result, the need for faith.

My greatest fear has always been failure. I'm not in denial. I'm acutely aware of my hesitancy to take a leap of faith when failure is an option. Too often I only take the leap with plan B, C, and D already mapped out. I've always got a contingency plan in place and will often overanalyze situations that require major decisions.

In 2008, my wife and I were in ministry positions we absolutely loved. Several of our friends in ministry had thought about planting a church and approached us about our interest. We knew we were called to plant a church at some point, but not now, and not in Tulsa, Oklahoma. I can vividly remember the car ride after meeting with our friends, where my wife and I were laughing at the thought of giving up our current ministry positions to plant a church in Tulsa. Six weeks later, after numerous sleepless nights and weeks of spiritual unrest, I knew God was up to something. He was changing my plans and timeline. Not only that, he was calling us to something that would require more faith than we'd ever had to exercise. This was leaving my security, my comforts, and my paycheck and stepping into something that would only happen by faith. There were no safety nets this time: no plan B and no contingency plans.

Years earlier one of my mentors gave me a book that I would read over and over again during moments of fear called *Ruthless Trust* by Brennan Manning. The reason this book helped me so much is because it didn't equate faith with clarity. Faith is stepping into the unknown and living by what we cannot see; it's learning to radically trust God every day with every step and every need.

Brennan Manning tells a story about the brilliant ethicist John Kavanaugh, who went to work for three months at the "house of the dying" in Calcutta, India. He was seeking a clear answer as to how best to spend the rest of his life, and on the first morning there he met Mother Theresa. She asked, "And what can I do for you?" Kavanaugh asked her to pray for him. "What do you want me to pray for?" she asked. He voiced the request that he had traveled thousands of miles from the United States to discover: "Pray that I have clarity." She said firmly, "No, I will not do that." When he asked her why, she said, "Clarity is the last thing you are clinging to and must let go of." When Kavanaugh commented that she always seemed to have the clarity he longed for, she laughed and said: "I have never had clarity; what I have always had is trust. So, I will pray that you trust God."[18]

As God was leading my wife and I through this time of transition and radical faith, I slowly began to loosen the grip on my need for clarity and answers. I began to see that my incessant desire to know was actually fueling my fear and discontent and that by letting go of my need for clarity I could actually rest. It's such a counterintuitive truth. How can the unknown actually bring rest? It's because the unknown now creates space for faith, a moment when we step away from the steering wheel and completely trust that God is in control of our situation.

Although I've come a long way, I'm still a recovering clarity addict myself; a planner by nature who is always thinking strategically about the next step. However, I learned it was "the unknown" that was actually fueling my passion for God and my heartfelt desire to know him.

> *The unknown can either fuel our fear of the future or fuel our trust in God. It was always the seasons of "process" that became the catalyst for where God was taking me next. I'm not denying the importance of planning or having a strategy; it's simply an understanding that God works beyond our comprehension and our best formulated strategies. When we're living a life of faith and begin led by the Holy Spirit, we must learn to hold our plans and future loosely.*

I'm always challenged when I read through the book of Acts or the Pauline epistles and see how often they moved out with a common mission but without many details. Paul's journey as detailed in Acts 16:6-10 shows us how they planned to travel to certain areas, but the Holy Spirit directed them beyond their designed itinerary to the place they needed to be: in this case, Macedonia. They trusted God with their preconceived agenda and willingly submitted to the change of plans along the way. Most of us, including myself, wouldn't imagine living our lives this way. We set our plans in stone, and only extreme circumstances would ever alter our course. Instead of submitting our future to God and allowing him to direct our paths as we walk, we lay out our future and pray that God will bless our plans.

But herein lies the problem: when we hold on tightly to our own plans, we inevitably face doubts when something doesn't go according to schedule. Maybe decisions paralyze us because we're so accustomed to already knowing what to do. Maybe God can't change our plans because we're not used to regularly submitting our itinerary to him. We're going to go to college, get a degree, meet a future spouse, get a good job with opportunities for advancement, have two well-behaved children, and pursue our dreams without any impediment. Sounds pretty good, huh? Except, that is far from reality. Something inevitably interrupts our dreams, our plans, our schedule. What if we invited the interruptions into our lives as God guiding our steps, instead of something that derails us from our destination? What if the interruptions are necessary for faith?

When our future and our plans are not fully surrendered to God, we will struggle when things don't go according to our plan. But a life of predictability, one without challenges or obstacles, does not require radical faith. If our lives were a smooth, linear journey, we would never live in the joy that is only found through walking by faith. We falsely assume that a life of comfort, convenience, and predictability is what we really want, but that life is an illusion; it has the appearance of joy, but it is always lacking true substance. Instead, let us choose a life of radical faith, being led by the Holy Spirit and holding our plans with palms open.

Embrace the Mystery

My Lord God, I have no idea where I am going. I do not see the road ahead of me. I cannot know for certain where it will end.

> *Nor do I really know myself, and the fact that I think I am following your will does not mean that I am actually doing so. But I believe that the desire to please you does in fact please you. And I hope I have that desire in all that I am doing. I hope that I will never do anything apart from that desire. And I know that if I do this you will lead me by the road, though I may know nothing about it. Therefore, I will trust you always, though I may seem lost and in the shadow of death. I will not fear, for you are ever with me, and you will never leave me to face my perils alone.*
> *-Thoughts on Solitude by Thomas Merton.* [19]

What happens to your faith when God simply doesn't make sense? When all your understanding, all your learning, all your degrees and experience doesn't provide you with the clarity you need to navigate what lies before you? Unfortunately, so often the theological foundation we gained as a child or in our churches doesn't adequately prepare us for these challenges of faith.

I was six years into biblical and theological studies before I learned a word that would forever change the trajectory of my faith: MYSTERY! It's not a word many academics have the confidence to use. On numerous occasions Paul uses the word "mystery" to describe this incredible revelation of "Christ in us." We use "mystery" when we describe the power of the Eucharist and coming to the table, or when we describe the beautiful covenant of marriage where two people become one, or when we describe the power of baptism as we immerse ourselves in the death and life of Jesus. As I began to pour over the works of some of the great Christian mystic writers, my heart was captured by a God who didn't have to be measured, weighed, or put on trial for every action or discrepancy. I had watched too many friends and colleagues make the slow journey away from a personal relationship with Christ because of unreconciled discoveries in their theological reflection. I began to realize that I didn't need more certitudes in my life; I needed more mystery.

I can vividly remember sitting in my dorm room as an undergraduate student in biblical studies talking to a friend of mine who was about to embark on a journey to Yale Divinity School. He summarized his last few years of study as a long, arduous journey from a faith that could be categorized, labeled, and packaged to one that was now in need of defense. His faith had once seemed so simple and straightforward, and now many of the complexities of theological examination had him confused and questioning some of the major pillars of belief. He had successfully distanced himself from the greater story of God—the salvation history that is at work through the writings of scripture—, and he had magnified the unreconciled issues of his faith into massive boulders standing in the middle of his path. That night he made the declaration, as a result of his theological journey and personal experiences, that he could believe Jesus to be a great teacher, but not Lord and Savior.

I grew up in the Pentecostal/Charismatic movement. My great-grandfather and grandfather were both Assembly of God ministers, and I'm deeply appreciative of many things that were passed onto me. I've learned it's not always necessary to throw out the baby with the bathwater, and the importance of "eating the meat and spitting out the bones" applies to almost every arena of life. You don't have to dismiss an idea or person just because you find an area of disagreement.

Growing up in this movement, however, led many of us to believe that clarity equaled a closer walk with Christ. If you were really in tune with the Holy Spirit, then he would be speaking to you so clearly that it would be impossible to miss God's will or the direction for your life. This isn't intended to dismiss the role of the prophet in the church or the ability of the Holy Spirit to bring clarity in our lives; instead, it's addressing the false belief that every issue has a formula and every problem can be traced back to a deficiency in our faith.

There was always an answer, even if we had to make it up right there on the spot and adorn it with some spiritual jargon to make it slide down a little easier. Some of the most egocentric, non-biblical, manipulative statements I've ever heard in my life started with the phrase, "Thus sayeth the Lord..." We had somehow systematized the unknowable, attempting to limit the unfathomable mysteries of our faith to something we could grab onto. We like a faith with handles; something we can easily grab onto and turn as we need or as we find convenient.

Clarity is not altogether a bad thing. In fact, if you're leading an organization, trying to grow a department, or are a student with a study emphasis, some level of clarity is essential and healthy. The problem is when clarity becomes an idol and not a tool. The problem arises when we seek clarity at all costs and our faith becomes something we wield just to get more clarity.

I remember sitting in service after service listening to ministers say phrases like, "I was driving yesterday, and out of the blue God just spoke as clear as I'm speaking to you right now and said, _____." I must admit the cynic in me always wondered if they had truly learned to decipher God's voice so clearly. How easy life must be when there is nothing to be wrestled with or no mystery that goes unresolved. Maybe they really have learned to hear the voice of God that effortlessly, but the rest of us still wrestle with determining God's direction.

I've learned that this incessant drive to know or think we know can be a cheap facade for genuine faith. I've learned there is a richness, depth, and authenticity in the mystery of our faith that all the clarity in the world cannot surpass. Sitting in the struggle and wrestling with the uncertainty draws us back to a faith that is not rooted in what we can see or what we know, but instead, a deep, residing trust in the goodness and sovereignty of our Father.

Clarity can easily lead us to pride, while mystery must lead us back to him. I've also learned that I'm forced to sit in the mystery of my faith much more often than I have the benefit of clarity. As a recovering clarity addict myself, my prayer for you is that you find a depth and richness in the mystery of your faith that goes deeper than all the clarity you could ever imagine. That you begin to live in such a way that you relish the mystery of your faith, because in that moment there is no response other than to lean in a little bit closer.

CHAPTER 9

Through the Wall

Doubters Club

I have a heart for people who struggle with doubt. For whatever reason, I've always been drawn to them, and it comes out in the way I teach, pastor, and lead our church. It probably stems from growing up in an environment where asking real questions was frowned upon. It's almost as if God were fragile and anything that pushed the boundaries of what is normal or orthodox sends you into the land of no return. As a result, we develop a faith that is fragile with so much bubbling just beneath the surface of our lives, just waiting to come up. We shove everything down a little deeper and deeper until one day, and usually in a moment of crisis or a cave experience, everything comes flooding out. In my experience, this scenario is rarely healthy. What is healthy is learning to be honest with yourself, with God, and with others. Instead of trying to find the right words to say, we can just pray what is really on our hearts—as if we're really capable of keeping something from God anyway. It has always astounded me why we try to pray as if there are certain things we can hide from God.

In fact, I believe doubt to be a necessary step on the journey of genuine faith. How can something be genuine if it's never been tested and proved? In his book *The Other Side of Silence,* Morton Kelley tells a story about a man who comes to a huge canyon, unable to cross to the other side. As the man stood, wondering what to do next, he was amazed to discover a tightrope stretched across the abyss. And slowly, surely, across the rope came an acrobat pushing before him a wheelbarrow with another performer in it. When they finally reached the safety of solid ground, the acrobat smiled at the man's amazement. "Don't you think I can do it again?" he asked. And the man replied, "Why, yes. I certainly believe you can." The performer put his question again, and when the answer was the same, he pointed to the wheelbarrow and said, "Good! Then get in and I will take you across."[20]

At some point, faith requires that we get into the wheelbarrow and trust Jesus with our lives and our understanding. For so many people, their faith requires a combination of all the right things that will get them to the other side. Maybe it's a proper apologetic: a place where all our questions are neatly wrapped with a nice bow on top. Maybe it's having a proper belief system in place, where you confess the right things to get across. What we cannot escape in our spiritual journey is the reality that the Christian faith actually requires "faith." This doesn't discount at all the necessity of apologetics and proper theology; it simply acknowledges that Christianity is predicated on faith: believing in something we can't always see or quantify. So, at some point, what actually gets us from one side to the other is believing in the reality of the gospel and the work of Christ and how it has spiritually and physically changed our standing.

So, why do so many "church people" get upset when a nineteen-year-old begins to ask real questions about faith and God, but we have no problem when nearly half the book of Psalms does it? Over 40 percent of the Psalms are classified as laments; songs of great sorrow and grief, many of them questioning God's goodness or involvement or plan. In the first half of the book of Psalms, over 60 percent of the writings are songs of lament.

Look at the raw emotions of this song of David in Psalm 22:1-2, as he says, "My God, my God, why have you forsaken me? Why are you so far from saving me, so far from my cries of anguish? My God, I cry out by day, but you do not answer, by night, but I find no rest."

Think about these words for a minute. Now, go look at the top one hundred worship songs currently being circulated in our churches on a weekly basis. I guarantee you will find it difficult to find even one song of lament. In a culture where we would rather feel good about what we are reciting, we have altogether missed the power of lament and how it both heals our soul and draws us closer to God in a unique and profound way. Without it, we become machines, saying words and singing songs that don't truly reflect the internal struggle our souls are facing. Over time, without laments, we exchange the authentic cry of our hearts for a cheap façade and, subsequently, a sturdy faith for one that is delicate.

If you've ever experienced the profound freedom of confession, then I don't have to convince you of anything. You know firsthand why James implores the church in chapter 5 to "confess your sins one to another" so that you may be "healed." There is nothing altogether pleasant about the actual act of confession, and yet its effect can be like a wet blanket being lifted off your body and soul. It's like you've been living life in two feet of mud, trudging along, and someone sets you on solid ground for the first time. Have you ever taken the time to really stop and think about what you're doing each and every time you pray an honest prayer or practice the discipline of confession? You're exposing and disarming one of the enemy's greatest weapons. You are taking tools meant to keep you in spiritual denial and locked in a prison of your doubts, your past, and your shame and willingly humbling yourself to the point of exposure. You've disarmed pride, deceit, and a real spiritual darkness that exists.

Many of us have simply been lied to. We've been led to believe that prayers, songs, and hymns that question God's hand or sovereignty are unhealthy and have no place in the life of a believer. I believe David would sharply disagree. In fact, I believe one of the many factors that made David a man after God's own heart was his incredible ability to write songs of lament without letting go of the rope. How often in David's psalms to do you see him begin his song in a place of despair and utter disillusionment, but, as the song proceeds, the words of honesty and confession become like a salve applied to his own soul?

In Psalm 13, David starts with: "How long, Lord? Will you forget me forever? How long will you hide your face from me? How long must I wrestle with my thoughts and day after day have sorrow in my heart? How long will my enemy triumph over me?" After a few more verses, here's how he ends this chapter. "But I trust in your unfailing love; my heart rejoices in your salvation. I will sing the Lord's praise, for he has been good to me." Herein lies the power of David's song and prayer. It combines both the authenticity of what he is feeling in this particular circumstance with the truth of who he knows God to be.

These blatant expressions of doubt and lack of understanding actually lead him into the deeper mystery of faith. They lead into incredible declarations about God's unchanging character and his endless love on behalf of his people. Sometimes you simply need to talk yourself into what you actually believe. Sometimes confession precedes belief, and sometimes we confess ourselves into belief. By practicing confession, we are unmasking the plan of the enemy to keep the doubt hidden, neatly tucked away in the recesses of our faith where there seems to be no place for such discussions.

Psalm 57 gives us the song that David sang while in the cave on the run for his life. I believe that only an individual who has learned their identity while in the pasture will be able to sing this song while in the cave.

> *Have mercy on me, my God, have mercy on me,*
>
> *for in you I take refuge.*
>
> *I will take refuge in the shadow of your wings*
>
> *until the disaster has passed.*
>
> *I cry out to God Most High,*
>
> *to God, who vindicates me.*
>
> *He sends from heaven and saves me,*
>
> *rebuking those who hotly pursue me—*
>
> *God sends forth his love and his faithfulness.*
>
> *I am in the midst of lions;*
>
> *I am forced to dwell among ravenous beasts—*
>
> *men whose teeth are spears and arrows,*

> *whose tongues are sharp swords.*
>
> *Be exalted, O God, above the heavens;*
>
> *let your glory be over all the earth.*
>
> *They spread a net for my feet—*
>
> *I was bowed down in distress.*
>
> *They dug a pit in my path—*
>
> *but they have fallen into it themselves.*
>
> *My heart, O God, is steadfast,*
>
> *my heart is steadfast;*
>
> *I will sing and make music.*
>
> *Awake, my soul!*
>
> *Awake, harp and lyre!*
>
> *I will awaken the dawn.*
>
> *I will praise you, Lord, among the nations;*
>
> *I will sing of you among the peoples.*
>
> *For great is your love, reaching to the heavens;*
>
> *your faithfulness reaches to the skies.*
>
> *Be exalted, O God, above the heavens;*
>
> *let your glory be over all the earth.*

True brokenness leads us to the most honest prayers. We don't feel the need to hide or to say the perfect words or to even make our theology fit perfectly. I can only imagine how the cave experience changed the way David prayed.

What would change about your prayers if instead of getting promoted to CEO of your company, you were let go, labeled a traitor, and forced to leave everything you knew and loved in search of something new?

The Road to Emmaus

I'm incredibly thankful that scripture doesn't leave out the messy stories. We may have a hard time with doubt and spiritual skepticism, but it was apparent that God often led those he called through seasons of uncertainty. It was a necessary process.

In Luke 24, we see two disciples walking home from Jerusalem along the road to Emmaus. The Passover had ended, and Jesus had been crucified. This was the ultimate walk of shame. They had given their lives to this Jesus movement, believing him to be the Messiah. Now they had to go back home, and what did they have to show for it? They "had hoped he was the one to redeem Israel" (Luke 24:21), but this now seemed to be nothing more than a fantasy.

I can only imagine the conversation along the road ranging from, "But we saw him perform the miracles," to, "I truly believed him to be the one." They had walked to Jerusalem with so much anticipation and belief, the seven-mile walk back home must have been the longest day of their lives.

What do you do when God disappoints? What do you do when God doesn't live up to your expectations or doesn't show up like you want? A week earlier these followers of Jesus were laying their cloaks and palm branches on the ground, inaugurating their Messiah and King, who they believed would overthrow the Roman government and establish his kingdom.

The events of Easter week would disappoint the crowd, disappoint the disciples, and disappoint those closest to Jesus. Jesus simply didn't show up like they wanted or expected. But we know that in the midst of their greatest disappointment, God was doing something so much greater and superior to anything they could begin to comprehend. Can you believe this same thing for your life? When God has seemed to disappoint, could it be that God is up to something more?

> *As the two men were walking along the road to Emmaus, Jesus showed up and began to walk with them. I want you to stop and think about the implications of this for a minute. They were walking away from Jerusalem; away from belief, and away from the crucifixion and possibility of resurrection. AND JESUS WAS WALKING WITH THEM. Just like the disciples, you may not recognize him, but he is walking with you – even in your unbelief.*

Most of us will walk down our own road to Emmaus at some point in our lives. Whether it's the result of pain or circumstances, or getting wounded by someone we love, or simply that our faith no longer makes sense—and yet Jesus walks with us. He intentionally conceals his identity from these disciples because he wants them to make a discovery. Jesus speaks truth into their lives and confirms what he and the prophets had spoken about the necessity of suffering.

Often on the road to Emmaus we experience the painful, yet necessary process of deconstruction. We begin to dismantle a faith that no longer makes sense or a faith that was built upon our circumstances. Just like Jesus did to the disciples on this road, he begins to speak truth into the lies we have held and believed. He uncovers and exposes how we have easily built the foundation of our faith upon our own understanding, and not on the unchanging and immovable hope we have in Christ. We learn how the way of Christ is the way of the cross and that our road will require pain, but it is serving a greater and bigger purpose.

That evening around the table Jesus broke the bread and gave it them, and their eyes were opened. I love how this revelation took place at the table. That through the Eucharist they were able to see who Jesus was, understand who they were, and realize the implications of a risen Messiah.

"And they rose that same hour and returned to Jerusalem." (Luke 24:33)

Maybe the only way to get to Jerusalem is through Emmaus. It may not make sense geographically, but it's the way of Jesus. He takes us through seasons of searching and discovery that we might find him: not some false imitation or cheap knockoff, but something real. Something that allows us to begin rebuilding, this time upon the rock, not the sand.

I've spent a long time along the road to Emmaus. I've wrestled and struggled and deconstructed. I've experienced disillusionment with the Christian faith, a disappointment from discovering something is not as good as you believed it to be. And now I've just begun to see how God was drawing me out in order to draw me back in.

The Power of Confession

It's not *if* you experience brokenness, it's *when*. Pull back the curtain on every person, every leader, every pastor or spiritual leader, and you will find some level of brokenness. Something they've gone through, something they're going through, or something they're still learning to process.

I believe that brokenness, whether it is inflicted on ourselves because of sin or given to us through the circumstances of life, confronts us with a choice. Do we go into hiding like Adam and Eve, or do we practice the art of excruciating vulnerability?

In 2010, Brene Brown gave a TED Talk on vulnerability that is still one of the most viewed TED Talks of all time. She talked about one of our greatest fears: Is there something about me, that if other people know it or see it, will eliminate me from connection? She says in order for real, genuine connection to happen, we must be willing to practice excruciating vulnerability. Vulnerability is at the core of shame and fear and our struggle for worthiness, but it is also the birthplace of joy, love, creativity, belonging, etc.[21]

There is a reason Alcoholics Anonymous has been such an effective program for so many decades. There is something healthy, and deeply spiritual, about creating an environment where brokenness is both embraced and confessed. Nobody feels the need to hide, because you don't come to AA meetings if your life is neat and clean. The entire program is predicated upon this understanding of confession and owning the brokenness that lies just beneath the surface of our lives. You don't need to hide, because nobody else is hiding. It's one of the very few safe places where you don't have to pretend.

We are often deceived into believing that the consequences of confession are greater than the consequences of concealment. We are willing to experience a lifetime of hiding in the shadows and living under the weight of our pain, instead of risking the possibility of potential rejection from others: a rejection that often only lives in our minds and never becomes reality.

The problem is that we're good at hiding. It's a part of our sinful nature. In Genesis 3:7-11, nobody has to teach Adam and Even to cover their nakedness and to hide from the presence of God. It is a natural response to shame, guilt, and condemnation.

It's possible that if David's brothers and family hadn't heard about David hiding out in the Cave of Adullam, he would have just gone deeper and deeper into the cave, attempting to bury the pain and disappointment and embarrassment he was facing. That would have been quite a natural response to such an issue.

> *I've learned firsthand over the years how the enemy is constantly trying to get me all alone. Attempting to push me into the dark corners of isolation, where I can easily be misled and deceived. The Holy Spirit, however, is constantly leading me towards the light, to deeper places of being known and to a greater level of vulnerability and confession.*

I often think about what the church would look like if we let go of all our false pretenses, put down our masks, and were willing to embrace our own personal brokenness. The freedom that could be experienced by the people who sit in the seats every week at church. How those outside the church would look in and see a bunch of people who have owned their sin and brokenness and are in a process of being redeemed by the work of the gospel. Hiding keeps us in bondage and ultimately leads us into a life of duplicity. In fact, without an honest assessment of our brokenness and a willingness to practice confession, we are forced into a life of hypocrisy. It's inevitable that we become the Pharisee or religious leader Jesus repeatedly calls out in the Sermon on the Mount.

Here's a place in the book where it would be much easier to tell a fictional story or tell you about one of 1,000 different people over the years who have confessed to me in a group or in my office. But I'm going to tell you a personal story. A part of my story that is still a little bit raw and something that God is increasingly bringing out of the shadows and into the light.

In November 2014, I took a trip to Honduras to visit one of our sister churches and a child project development center we help run. I'd taken this trip numerous times over the years. One evening, in the middle of the night, I woke up extremely sick. I spent the rest of the evening on the bathroom floor with my face pressed against the cold tile. The next day I tried to get it together and took some nausea medicine so I could stand up that evening and preach for our sister church. It was ninety-five degrees with about 90 percent humidity. It was the worst sermon of my life, but I survived.

When I returned home, I took the normal medication to kill off any parasites or worms that I may have ingested, but I only continued to get worse. Over the next several months I visited four different doctors, gastroenterologists, and specialists who did every scope, diet change, and test imaginable. It got to the point where I had lost over twenty pounds and was sick every single day. I would take nausea medicine every Sunday morning just so I could preach all three Sunday morning services at City Church. I was praying, other people were praying, we were doing everything we knew how to do, but nothing was working.

During this time, I went to a dark place, emotionally, spiritually, and physically. I had never suffered from a major physical ailment, and it absolutely broke me down in every possible way. I let on to my wife and some of my closest friends that things were difficult, but I masked how bad it really was. I told myself I had to be strong and could make it through and that if I just kept going, there eventually would be relief. I felt mad. I felt abandoned. I felt guilty. I felt powerless.

I was sick every day for almost two years. A friend of ours recommended a naturopathic doctor in town who had a special technique for finding digestive problems. Honestly, by this point I would have probably drunk a magic potion off the street if I thought there was any chance of relief. I visited this doctor, and within three hours she called me back. She told me I had an extremely rare type of parasite that often doesn't respond to medications we have in the United States. The parasite had grown to be over a foot long in my large intestines and somehow had gone completely undetected in every scan or test. Not only was it stealing my best nutrients, but it had all but destroyed my thyroid gland, the part of the body responsible for developing so many key hormones for the body and digestive system. That day I started a one-year road to recovery: killing off the parasite, passing it through my system (yes, just like you think), and then rehabilitating my system to produce the right chemicals and hormones again.

What I'm about to tell you next is not a theology I've developed or something I'm telling you to do. It's my story and my response to the leading of the Holy Spirit.

I wrestled with guilt because I believed there were parts of my life I had kept hidden from my wife and some of those closest to me. I thought I was protecting my wife, but really it was my pride telling me that I had it under control. How often does the Enemy's greatest tactic in our life start with the phrase, "I've got this under control!" I told myself that my wife was at home with our three small children (and one on the way) and that she couldn't carry my burden as well. Not only did I experience the pain and darkness of dealing with the sickness, but also the guilt of some personal sin I had allowed into my life during this time. It was both the weight of things I couldn't control and of things I had allowed to control me.

All the while, God had brought a group of men into my life who were also pastors and church leaders who had gone or were going through intense brokenness and were now on the other side of confession and healing. I opened up my soul to them. I saw their freedom and joy, and I inwardly longed to experience the same. But that pride deep down inside of us often convinces us that the consequences of confession are greater than the consequences of living in darkness. Nothing could be further from the truth. I've learned that while the enemy has no control over us, he will continue to feed us lies because that's all he has to offer. And if we believe the lie, then we lock ourselves up in the chains of bondage and untruth.

I can still remember this night so vividly. It is simultaneously one of the worst and greatest nights of my life. I woke up at 2:30 a.m. wide awake, something that rarely happens to me. Only one other time in my life had I felt the leading and weight of the Holy Spirit like I did in this moment. It was very clear: "You need to confess to your wife what you have been carrying." That night I woke her up from a deep sleep, and I told her what I had been carrying for the last two years. At least, I told her 98 percent of it. There was 2 percent that was still too difficult.

The next night I woke up at 2:30 a.m. again. The same leading of the Holy Spirit from the night before, and the message was clear: "Now tell her the last 2 percent."

I wept that night. A deep, gut-wrenching, soul-emptying cry. It was two years of pain and suffering and darkness and secrecy that came flooding out. We can't even begin to understand the weight we carry when we choose to live in isolation, darkness, and fear. Often, this weight isn't truly realized until we experience it being lifted from us. In that moment, we realize what we've been carrying the whole time and how it's kept us from experiencing life to the fullest.

It was simultaneously the most horrible and freeing experience of my life. I'm so blessed to have a strong wife of both love and grace who just held me and allowed the work of the Holy Spirit to do what was necessary. It was difficult, but also a turning point in our lives and marriage. God taught me more than I could ever imagine through that deep brokenness. I had been humbled by both life and my choices, but I had also experienced the unconditional love of my heavenly Father, my wife, and some great men of God. It's why we often look back at our cave moments with both sorrow and joy. We wouldn't trade what God has done for anything, and yet we also have no desire to relive the pain.

Do you know one of the things I learned from this? That the Holy Spirit is ALWAYS leading me into deeper places of freedom and life, not comfort or temporary happiness. The deep joy that is found in confession and being fully known is always greater than the deception of the enemy that says, "Nobody can ever know," or, "You can handle this on your own!"

It's often in the deeply broken places of your life where you realize you cannot do it on your own. You can't manage your life, and you are completely incapable of fixing the deeply broken places of your soul. And the only real response to this revelation is surrendering everything you are to him and leaning heavily on the men and women of God you have placed in your life. You even come to realize that so much of the pain is actually GRACE!

I recently sat with a small group of pastors as we were working toward a strategy for church multiplication. The host pastor, whose church had been ranked #1 in *Outreach Magazine*'s fastest growing churches issue the year before, began telling the story of his church. After he concluded, there was a short time of Q&A. One of the pastors in our group asked the question, "How do you stay grounded and rooted when you've experienced so much notoriety and success over the past year?"

As he started talking, his voice cracked, tears filled his eyes, and he needed a few seconds to regain his composure. He began telling the story of his very first year as a church planter, when he lost his way. That in a two-month span, he spent only a handful of evenings at home with his family. One day when he came home, his wife and kids had packed up their things and gone to stay with their family, because he had clearly chosen the church over them. Through tear-filled eyes, he told us that in that moment he realized that he had lost everything that really mattered to him. Ministry would not be his mistress or his idol; he would commit to being a healthy leader, pastor, and husband. And you know what? I believed him.

Some might say that they don't want to follow a leader who has walked through brokenness, whether inflicted on themselves or something out of their control. I've learned, however, quite the opposite. It's a leader who has visited the cave and walked out with a greater understanding of their brokenness and their desperate need for a Savior, who is now prepared for what lies ahead in the palace.

It's one thing to know about grace and an entirely different thing to experience it. The cave empties us and prepares us, not for the life we thought we would live, but for the life we've inwardly longed for the whole time—to be both fully known and fully loved.

PART III: THE PALACE

> *"All the tribes of Israel came to David at Hebron and said, 'We are your own flesh and blood. In the past, while Saul was king over us, you were the one who led Israel on their military campaigns. And the Lord said to you, "You will shepherd my people Israel, and you will become their ruler."' When all the elders of Israel had come to King David at Hebron, the king made a covenant with them at Hebron before the Lord, and they anointed David king over Israel. David was thirty years old when he became king, and he reigned forty years. – 2 Samuel 5:1-4*

The palace can be an amazing place. It can be a place where our dreams, God's call, and years of preparation collide, as we begin to live out God's unique mission for our life.

For David, the process of the pasture, the cave, and years of leading a band of fugitives had prepared him for the palace. The reality, however, is that not everyone makes it to the palace, and for those who do, sometimes it's nothing like they imagined. Our place of convergence can be an amazing place, but only if we have fully embraced the obscurity of the pasture and the lessons of brokenness that are only learned in the cave.

Scripture never tells us this specifically, but I can only imagine there were moments when King David would venture out to the open fields just north of Jerusalem and reminisce about his time as a shepherd. The moments when he fought off the lion and the bear. The countless thousands of stones he put in his slingshot and fired toward a small bush or tree stump. The hundreds of Psalms and prayers that originated in that empty space. In fact, it's possible that David missed those days in the pasture where life was a little simpler and expectations were far less consuming. Do you think he went back and visited the Cave of Adullum years later? Remembering what it was like walking into that cave thinking your life was over and walking out leading a group of rebels. When we are given the luxury of hindsight, it's rather remarkable and usually unmistakable how God's hand has guided us to our present circumstance.

The pasture is a required stop on our journey. Without a firm identity, we won't know who we are. The cave is not only an absolute necessity but also a definite certainty in our lives. Without being surrendered and broken, we will never learn to live and lead like Jesus.

The palace also reveals something extremely vital: *If God wasn't enough for you in the pasture, he will never be enough for you in the palace.* Your wildest desires could come true, only to find out that you are just as discontent as you were before. This is why it is so crucial we don't shortcut or skip our season of development. Here's the kicker. Here's the piece that must keep us grounded in him. Identity and character are rarely formed in the palace; they're only revealed.

The palace actually presents us with a side of David that we haven't seen up to this point. We see his failures. We see pride, lust, and deception fill the heart of our great king. We also see him operating as "a man after the heart of God" and as the greatest king that Israel, and possibly the world, had ever seen. The palace is not some sort of fairyland place where everything is now perfect and we just get to ride into the sunset. The palace is still a place where we must remember who we are and where we still experience the brokenness of life. It's where we implement the lessons learned in the pasture and the cave.

If the pasture was about IDENTITY and the cave about SURRENDER, then I believe the palace is about PURPOSE.

In this next section, I want to clarify purpose. Purpose is not how much you do or the magnitude of your calling, it's walking in faithfulness and obedience out of a deep, abiding relationship with Christ. It's choosing to bring glory to God and choosing to make God's kingdom a reality here on earth wherever you go. And you can't fake or manufacture this. You can't produce it on your own. Your true purpose will only flow out of your identity in Christ. It's not something that can be found as we wander the streets of life searching for some elusive idea that will bring us meaning.

As we noted in Part I of this book, God has given each of us a first-order calling and a second-order calling. If we fail to understand the difference or fail to keep these callings in order, then we will find ourselves in grave trouble. We've spent the majority of Part I and Part II discussing our first-order calling: living in an intimate relationship with God through Christ. Part III now delves into how our first-order and second-order callings begin working in unison, using the gifts God has developed in us to reach people and make disciples.

The issue we will wrestle with is that we inevitably want to pass over our first-order calling in the hope that our second-order calling will somehow bring us what we desire. It doesn't. It can't. What we do for God must be birthed out of our relationship with him.

I believe God wants us to move into the palace in our lives. The palace is a great thing. It's simply imperative that we take the pasture and the cave with us. Let's see how our main character does at fulfilling his purpose now that the palace—the result of years of work—has been realized.

CHAPTER 10

The Secret

No Matter What

Don't be discouraged if your purpose doesn't seem as spectacular as a palace. Very few will ever be able to compare their calling to the life of King David. It's not about the scope or the amount of people or the grandeur surrounding your calling, it's about living out of the overflowing abundance of Christ in you: allowing him to use your story to impact others. It's about walking in faithfulness and obedience to the calling that has been placed on your life.

As we've navigated this book, we've taken actual physical places in the life of David and made them metaphors for the seasons we experience on our spiritual journey. I want to make it absolutely clear that although David experienced an actual physical palace, first in Hebron and later in Jerusalem, I don't believe the pinnacle of your spiritual journey needs to have a physical location or an official job title. It's learning that when you embrace God's process for your life, he inevitably begins to lead you to places where you begin to use your life in service to others. In fact, the pasture and the cave have usually refined us to the place where titles, positions, and status don't drive us like they once did.

I believe there is a level of spiritual maturity Christians can experience as they move into the palace. The pasture and the cave have taught and shaped them in such a profound way that now they have built a foundation that keeps them upright even amidst the storms of life. It reminds me of the story Jesus told about the man who builds his house on the sand or the rock. It's not only hearing the word, but by "putting it into practice" that the individual moves from a foundation that is in constant danger of being washed away, to a new foundation that can withstand the inevitable storms that will come their way (Matthew 7:24-27).

A person experiencing the palace is no longer controlled by the opinions of others, the treadmill of performance, or the detours of the destination; in fact, by this time they are prepared for the barrage of potential setbacks that might await them. Those setbacks don't paralyze them or cause them to drift off course, they are an inevitable part of living out God's purpose. The journey has prepared them and their faith has matured.

In college, I decided to take a mountain biking class. After a few weeks of riding, I was invited to take go on a three-day camping and mountain biking trip to some famous single-track trails in northwest Arkansas. Most of the people on my trip had been riding for several years, and I knew I would have some catching up to do. What I didn't realize was that in order to cover fifteen to twenty miles a day in the mountainous area we were riding, we would have to ride at a very quick pace. We were an hour into our ride, and I was struggling to keep up. Honestly, the fear of being left alone in the backwoods of Arkansas (insert banjo music playing) was the only thing motivating me from falling way behind. At our first break, I was riding up to the group who had already been sitting there for several minutes, and a look of pure exhaustion was all over my face. One of the more experienced riders came over to offer me some advice. "You'll never make it riding this way. You're trying to avoid every rock, every tree root, and every little hole on the trail. You have to learn to trust your bike so you can maintain your speed and conserve your energy. Instead of looking right in front of you, start trusting your bike, and start looking farther down the trail." It was good advice. I had to begin to learn to trust my bike so I could ride faster without becoming fatigued. It was amazing how much I improved as a mountain biker in just three days. With every pedal stroke I was gaining confidence.

I believe our journey to spiritual maturity looks a lot like this. Early in our journey we are looking at every single rock in front of us. The small things are big tests. We're learning how to trust God with our lives, our finances, and our future. As we grow in our faith, we realize that we can trust God with every single aspect of our lives, and we experience new levels of freedom and trust. Instead of allowing our financial situation to overwhelm us, we have learned that we can trust God to be our provider. We are allowing the trials and tests of life to shape and grow us. The pasture and cave have taught us these indispensable lessons.

If you've been exposed to scripture most of your life, then you might be tempted to simply read over a passage you've heard multiple times and not see it with fresh eyes, not allowing the Holy Spirit to illuminate something new to you. I think James 1:2-4 is one of those passages we may have read so many times that we don't really sit in the gravity of what it's saying to us.

"Consider it pure joy, my brothers and sisters, whenever you face trials of many kinds, because you know that the testing of your faith produces perseverance. Let perseverance finish its work so that you may be mature and complete, not lacking anything." (James 1:2-4)

Let's take just a minute to break down the implications of this passage. James is imploring us to find joy, deep-residing contentment, in the problems, pains, and afflictions that we all seek to avoid at any and all costs. Because as these tests come our way, they will teach us lessons in our faith that are absolutely essential to our spiritual formation: the understanding that only through tests and trials can we learn the lesson of perseverance—that's right, perseverance. Our faith is tested when we have to wait and scratch and persist in something that we cannot yet see or achieve. Faith becomes genuine when we continue to stand in something that hasn't yet happened. Faith is lived out when we have no other option than simply holding onto hope. And when we allow this "perseverance to finish its work" and we're still standing, we reach something James calls "maturity," and we become "complete," so now there's nothing that is "lacking" in us.

Think about the implications of this for a second. *If there is nothing that can knock you off course in life or nothing that can destroy your faith, is there anything you lack?* What an incredible place you are now living in. Your life and walk with Christ are no longer contingent on conditions or right circumstances, but now you are achieving the elusive "contentment" Paul refers to in Philippians 4:11. Oh, the irony of these verses. Only by letting go of all the things we think we need, do we begin experiencing the life we always desired. Only by experiencing delayed gratification and perseverance can we truly be thankful and content with what we've been given.

What we can't always see is what is happening in our lives below the surface. How our roots are spreading deeper and deeper into the ground. How the ground beneath us has somehow shifted from sand to stone: the perfect foundation for God to launch someone into their God-given purpose in life. And little do we know just how essential this will become in the place God is calling us to.

Never Enough

I absolutely loved studying history as a child. Growing up in Texas, I remember reading the story about a small group of Texas volunteers led by Davy Crockett, James Bowie, and William Travis, who took control of the Alamo and held off a massive Mexican force for thirteen days until they were finally overpowered.

That same year my family went on vacation to San Antonio. I remember walking along the streets downtown and then turning and standing before a white building. My dad looked at me and said, "There it is, son, that's the Alamo." I'm not sure what I expected, but it was more than what I got. This larger-than-life story that I loved studying was bigger than the incredibly average-looking, white structure that stood before me. I remember looking over at my dad with an underwhelmed look on my face and saying, "That's it? That's the Alamo?"

There is an allure of arriving at our desired destination. We fantasize about what it would be like to finally achieve what we've dreamed about. Unfortunately, the fantasy typically far outweighs the real experience. Many of us want to do whatever is necessary to get to the palace. We inwardly believe that the small, nagging desire for something more will finally be quenched in our souls. There are a lot of people who finally achieve their dream; they get the position, get married, get the vacation home, start the business, get the family they always wanted, but inwardly that nagging for something more doesn't leave. Why? Because it will never be enough.

Think about Adam and Eve for a moment. They had a place of perfection, uninterrupted fellowship with God, and a place where the work was not difficult or toilsome, but full of joy. And they gave it all away because they just had to know what the forbidden fruit was like. They had to know if they were missing out on something more. Adam and Eve get a bad rap, but I know my heart, and I know the hearts of humanity, and we are all "prone to wander," as the great hymn says. We are constantly searching for something else. The Garden of Eden was a place of perfection, and yet it wasn't enough for Adam and Eve. The sinful nature that is constantly at war with the Spirit of God in our lives is constantly whispering in our ear and telling us, "What you really need is right over there," or, "What you're experiencing right now is less than what it could be."

Because anything we do for God, any and all achievements that don't come from an abiding relationship with Christ, will force us back to a performance-based faith. And that path always leads to death, not life.

I've got a good friend who is a pastor. He's an extremely talented leader, speaker, and apologist. Every time I was around him he was planning and strategizing for ways to grow his church. All pastors I know do that to some extent, but this was a borderline obsession. He was constantly evaluating the numbers, the square footage, the growth barriers, and ways in which he could move the church forward. After several years of steady growth, they hit a large growth season in which their church grew to over 700 people in a small, 5,500 square foot facility. They decided to buy some property and start a giving campaign to build nearby. They easily raised the necessary money, and a little over a year later they moved into a beautiful, new, $4.5 million facility. By Easter, they had over 2,000 people attending their services.

After the initial rush of the new building subsided, I remember talking to him one day about what was next for him and the church. For the first time since I had known him, there was a general sense of uncertainty surrounding the church. He said that recently he just stood in the worship area for several minutes one day thinking about how this was the fulfillment of so many years of strategizing and hard work. I truly believe my friend has a strong relationship with Christ, but I think there was a sense of both satisfaction and disappointment that day as he stood in the worship area. Joy in the work that had been done, but disappointment in the reality that it didn't quite satisfy like he had hoped. The chase to get to this place had become like a drug, and now that it was attained, there was a natural letdown.

Wayne Muller in his book *Sabbath,* talks about the consequences of our endless pursuit for more.

The eschatology of progress is an inflated pyramid scheme, where our riches exist always to be mined and harvested in the future, through endlessly expanding markets, not here, not now, but there, and later, we will see the promised land, we will make the big score, our ship will come in, we will get the pot of gold at the end of the rainbow, our time will come, we will strike it rich, we will hit the jackpot, we will be on easy street. If the promised land is the good and perfect place, then where we are right now must be an imperfect place, a defective place. If the future is sacred, then the present is profane. Every day we are alive, every day we are not yet in paradise is a problem – our daily life is an obstacle in our way, it is another day short of the end time. Today – because it is not yet perfect – is always a bad day...Every time we finally reach the future, it vanishes in to the present. This perplexing tendency of the future to keep eluding us does not, of course, teach us to be more present, but rather to accelerate faster.[22]

I've learned from my own life that idols come in all kinds of shapes and sizes, and often come camouflaged in really "good" things that take the place of the "best" or "primary" things. Could it be that somewhere deep down inside, many of us are more obsessed with the gifts than the giver of those gifts? The dream than the giver of dreams? That we know how to wrap our idols up in pretty bows, so we can look at ourselves and justify the condition of our hearts? It becomes so easy to justify our idolatry when the end result is good things. But little do we realize that we are selling our souls: trading what is best for what is good.

There is absolutely nothing wrong with being driven or accomplishing great things or pursuing your dream; it's just that with these desires come the traps that lie to us and tell us that our accomplishments will complete us. I must admit that I've given into this lie on numerous occasions. Always believing that one more project, event, church plant, missions endeavor, or big Sunday will be what I've inwardly been searching for.

Tom Ashbrook, a spiritual formation coach and one of the leaders of Imago Christi, wrote a book called *Mansions of the Heart,* in which he explored the seven spiritual mansions first written about by Teresa of Avila in the 1500's. Although our spiritual lives are not a linear journey, the seven mansions described in his book take us on a journey of knowing Christ more intimately and allowing that intimacy to transform the way we live, worship, pray, serve, walk through struggles, etc.

Ashbrook notes that in our early spiritual mansions (Mansions 1 and 2), most Christians are focused on being Martha, on doing something significant with their lives for Christ. As we continue to grow, God will inevitably take us through a journey of truly understanding our identity: embracing what it means to be Mary sitting at the feet of Jesus. Mansions 3, 4, and 5 take us deeper into comprehending what an abiding relationship looks like. Sadly, most Christians never make it past Mansions 3 or 4. We get stuck in a repetitive cycle of not knowing who we are, and as a result, we go back to a work, performance-driven gospel.

In Mansions 6 and 7, not only are we truly experiencing the depth of learning to abide daily in Christ, but our spiritual lives are no longer dictated by the circumstances we're going through or the emotions we feel in our time with God. In Mansions 6 and 7, the individual has truly experienced a letting go of their life: a release of their agenda, their will, and their desires and are now willing to walk down whatever road God chooses to lay before them. But here is something I believe to be most significant. In Mansions 6 and 7, Mary and Martha learn to become one. Our life, ministry, service, passions, and abilities begin to flow out of a deep, abiding relationship with Christ. We're no longer driven by our own desire to achieve or a deep-seated need to perform for ourselves or for others. Instead, we begin to live our lives for Christ out of an overflowing security in him: a place of deep peace and joy that is founded on nothing other than him. Life for Christ begins to spill over from this life in Christ.[23]

> *I think this is what we really desire, whether we realize it or not. A place where Mary and Martha have merged. A place where kingdom living takes place from a kingdom heart. A place where obedience flows from the abundance of knowing Christ. Where the things we do for God don't define us, they are simply a joyous response of being sons and daughters. Something inside of us that naturally grows and no longer needs to be manufactured.*

I remember sitting in a three-day spiritual formation retreat several years ago listening about the mansions. I inwardly longed to experience what was described in Mansions 6 and 7. When you're an achievement addict like myself, it is so counterintuitive to begin thinking about productivity as sitting at the feet of Jesus. There are plans to be made, problems to be solved, issues to be addressed, places to go, and people to be reached. Even spiritual growth can easily become a list of things that need to be accomplished. And herein lies one of my greatest struggles in life. A struggle that I will more than likely fight until the day I die. Will I be content to forever struggle with an identity found in my performance, or will I learn to truly rest in the gospel? Can I learn to live a Mary life in a Martha world? Will I leave the kitchen to sit at the feet of Jesus, or will I assume my output is what really makes me worthy to be a son?

What I love about the gospel of Jesus Christ is that it is a bottomless well: a never-ending fountain from which we can always draw. As I continue to gaze upon the beauty of Christ and the work that was done on my behalf, I only come to a deeper realization of my sin, my idolatry, and the reality that sons and daughters do not earn the favor or love of their father. I'll spend the rest of my days both resting in and delving into the reality of this truth!

Eyes Wide Open

Years ago, as I was working with a leadership coach, he asked me the question, "What is God trying to get you to understand in this season of your life?" I couldn't answer the question in the moment. I wasn't really sure, to be honest. It had been such a busy season of life after recently moving to a new city and starting a new church, I hadn't really stopped much to think about it.

The following week when we met, he asked me the same question. My answer was really simple: "Love God, and enjoy the journey!" This was my answer not because I was excelling in this area, but because I had spent the last two or three years of my life continually focused on what was next. I never stopped, I never slowed down, and I rarely ever enjoyed the moment. There was always something else to be done, always a new problem to be solved, and always a new level to be attained. One of my greatest regrets planting a church is that I didn't celebrate with my team or our church nearly enough. I didn't know how to savor the moment, and I was caught in an endless cycle of chasing the next moment.

I ended up taping the phrase, "Love God and enjoy the journey," to the dashboard of my car. It became a daily reminder that no amount of achievement or accolades will ever be enough. There is not some sort of secret destination just around the corner where your soul finally feels satisfied. In fact, the achievement can become a drug that strings you along and gives you a sense of purpose, only to leave you longing for something more.

That's why I've always believed Matthew 11:25-34 to be so incredibly subversive in light of how we see life. We know that trials and tribulations will come our way and we know that the road of discipleship will require sacrifice and possible persecution, but in the midst of this all, Jesus invites us into a new way of living. He invites us "not to worry" and to be like the flowers of the field that "do not labor or spin." And then in a statement that seems almost too basic, he tells us to "seek first his kingdom and his righteousness and all these things will be given to you as well." So what exactly are "all these things" that we will be given? All the things that we are currently worried about: what will we eat, what we will wear, and how it will all happen. The unknowns and the things we can't control. What an invitation!

Every summer I take my family to the mountains of Colorado to escape the triple-digit temperatures of July in Oklahoma, and we stay in a cabin owned by some of my family. With four small children, there is nothing easy about making a twelve-hour drive, especially through the nothingness that is Oklahoma, Kansas, and eastern Colorado. My wife and I have to prepare both physically and mentally for what will inevitably be a long, long drive. It never fails that no more than thirty minutes into a twelve-plus hour journey, one of our kids will ask, "How much longer?" My wife and I just look at each other, laugh, and reply, "You better get comfortable back there!"

I make it my goal in life to get us to the cabin in Colorado with the least resistance, the least number of stops, and with as little conflict as humanly possible. In the middle of all of that, I can actually become quite obsessed with arriving. So much so that I make my kids pee in a bottle or almost run out of gas trying to make a single tank go as far as humanly possible. I watch people stopping at these rest stops or playgrounds along the side of the highway, and I think to myself, "What kind of idiot actually stops to get out and have a picnic or let their kids play on the playground?" That's major minutes wasted from getting to wherever you're going. (I know, it's a sickness I have.) About two years ago, my wife and I decided to try something radical. We decided to stop overnight at a hotel around the halfway mark of the trip and let the kids swim for a few hours. I actually discovered that not only did we feel less rushed, but it made the entire trip more enjoyable because we took the time to stop, play, and rest.

Here is a simple, yet profound truth. When your eyes are set only on the destination, you miss everything that happens on the journey! Not just the difficult moments, but also and especially the beautiful moments. You're so locked in or driven or passionate that you miss life, you miss the people right in front of you, and you miss the beauty of God's goodness that can be found in everything. I'm learning to stop, to be present with the people I love the most, and to give them my very best. I'm learning that slowing down brings life. I'm learning that pausing and truly enjoying the moment makes all of life just a little bit sweeter.

FOMO

I believe finding true contentment in life is a challenge, but I must admit that with our technological advancements and the sheer amount of opportunities at our fingertips in the twenty-first century, it's become even more difficult. It's been fascinating to read how the concept of FOMO (Fear of Missing Out) is a very real phobia that is greatly impacting our younger generations. I used to joke about FOMO and think it was just a childish notion about people who always want to be the center of attention or the life of the party. I've since realized it's actually paralyzing a whole generation of young people and affecting almost every area of their spiritual lives.

Because they are always connected through social media, there is a constant fear of missing a connection, missing a social outing, or missing some sort of opportunity—even if that opportunity doesn't even exist. It's even created an inability for some to commit to a long-term relationship or marriage because of the fear of committing to something and missing out on something better.

Here is the really scary part: It doesn't matter how good life is right now or how great their experiences are in the moment, they're still fearful that they could be missing out on something far better. They're constantly connected, even unable to put down their phone and go to sleep at night because of the possibility of missing something.

For example, you can be on vacation experiencing the beauty of Glacier National Park, the pristine lakes, the mountain peaks, and the massive glaciers moving through the valleys, and the whole time you're looking down on your phone, seeing what your friend Ethan did on his trip to Walmart today. Our brains are being rewired, and we don't even realize it. To be honest, until I started instituting a social media fast several times a year, I was somewhat unaware of the grip it had taken on my own heart. My soul had been gripped by the comparison game, the temptation to project more than I am, and the constant need to stay connected. I realized how much of my everyday life was motivated by what I was projecting to others on social media.

The repercussions of this are multi-faceted, but more than anything it affects our ability to ever truly be content. How can you truly savor the moment or enjoy what is happening in the present when there is a constant voice saying, "You might be missing out!" or, "The grass is always greener on the other side, there's always more than what you're experiencing right now, stay connected 24/7, or you could miss out." These constant messages bombarding us have created profound discontentment.

I absolutely love that Paul uses the word *myéomai*, translated "secret" or "mystery," in Philippians 4:12. The word has connotations of learning the secret of something through personal experience. Paul had to learn through personal experience this incredible secret of contentment regardless of changing circumstances.

In arguably the most misunderstood and misused scripture in the entire Bible, Philippians 4:13, Paul clearly lays out how the power of Christ has empowered him to do "all things." Unfortunately, this isn't simply the blank check most of us think it is. I'm not sure if writing it on your shoes will make you play better in the fourth quarter with two minutes left on the clock, or if getting it tattooed on your lower back will help you beat out the other twelve applicants for the job promotion you want. I do know that Paul had discovered this "secret," this remarkable phenomenon where our lives do not dance to the rhythm of our circumstances. We are no longer enslaved by the highs and lows that accompany living in a world of both light and darkness.

This "secret" of contentment, through the empowerment of Christ in him, allowed him to remain tethered to something unchanging in the midst of a life in constant flux. There may not be a better picture of spiritual maturity than the people who have learned to live in relationship with Christ no matter the external factors surrounding them. That's why it's described as a "secret": a mystery that can only be discovered through deep reflection, understanding, revelation, and actual real-life experience. Paul learned it through experiencing these highs and lows. He disciplined his heart and mind to stay tethered to the hope he has in Christ, even when he found himself without food for three days.

I believe at some point in your faith journey, every person either becomes a cynic or a mystic. A cynic is someone who has been wounded and allowed the events and unknowns of life to corrode their confidence in the goodness of God. Instead of leaning into the pain or the unknown, they allow the seeds of distrust to be sewn in their hearts. A mystic is someone whose faith goes beyond a set of beliefs or theological doctrines and who no longer believes it is necessary to "know" or "explain" everything that comes their way. Through relationship with Christ, they can believe in his goodness, even when they fail to see or understand it. In fact, we could easily conclude that all mystics are simply "recovering cynics" who at some point decided to move toward God when they could have easily stepped away.

I've always found it quite remarkable when reading Pauline literature how someone with such a high-level calling experienced such intense persecution and suffering. Our western, consumer-driven mindset leads us to believe that anyone receiving such revelations from God would be immune or impervious to such difficulties. And yet, here is one of our great apostles who finds himself shipwrecked, beaten, hungry, abandoned, and left to deal with a "messenger from Satan," where only God's grace would be sufficient (2 Corinthians 12). Again, in 1 Timothy 6:6, Paul writes, "But godliness with contentment is great gain." Paul implores us to develop an attitude of the heart and mind that is completely independent of external factors and fully dependent on God.

A heart that is content in Christ isn't a searching heart. We feel no need to chase down something new or something better or receive our fix from how people perceive us or how many "likes" we've received. This, however, will require a great deal of discipline on your part. It will take a rewiring of how you think and live. Let's start today: Whatever you're doing today or whoever you're with, be there 100 percent in the moment. Put down your phone and be content with where you're at, whether you like it or not.

CHAPTER 11

Success

True Success

In the palace, we need a proper definition of success. In his book Visioneering, Andy Stanley says: "We confuse success with the rewards of success. Success is remaining faithful to the process God has laid out for you. The rewards of success are the raise, the promotion, the recognition, a happy home, wonderful children, etc. Those show up later. Unfortunately, we often don't consider ourselves successful until we experience the rewards." He goes on to explain how so many people give up on their dreams or face discouragement because they confuse success with the rewards of success.[24] David wasn't successful just when he became king of Israel in 2 Samuel 5 or when he defeated an army. He was equally successful when he faithfully showed up for his job as shepherd boy in 1 Samuel 16.

If we don't redefine success, then we set ourselves up for disappointment and revert back to an identity that is not based on who we are in Christ but on a performance-based philosophy; something all the "success" in the world cannot fill. There will always be somebody who can outperform us or who has a God-given talent or ability we wish we had. If success is simply being the "best" or achieving the "most," then we will experience a radical insecurity when we fail to achieve those standards.

I've been a full-time pastor for almost fourteen years now. I've read the books, attended the conferences, and sat around with other pastors talking about the "wins" of ministry. It becomes very clear that "success" for a pastor is relegated to your attendance on Sunday morning and, if we're honest, usually your Easter attendance. I've jokingly told my closest pastor friends that if you're going to publicize your Easter attendance, you must also publicize your Memorial Day weekend attendance. That's guaranteed to keep us humble!

As a result of our obsession with large numbers, we put the people with the largest churches on the pedestal or give them the microphone at the conferences. We assume that they've unlocked the secret the rest of us have been frantically searching for and now they're going to let us in. I have no problem at all with megachurches or the people who pastor those churches. I have a problem when we have redefined "success" in the church arena to the people who can put the most people in a room, regardless of those individuals becoming disciples at all.

Sometimes success is faithfulness, and sometimes success is believing for something that you never get to see. Sometimes success is planting thousands of seeds that someone else is going to harvest, and sometimes it's plowing a field your whole life just to see another person reap the benefits. Sometimes success is remaining unknown and inconspicuous and sometimes it's praying and building a relationship over time to see one person come to discipleship to Jesus.

Hebrews 11 said that some of the greatest people of faith never got to witness the miracle or the fulfillment of the promise in this life. The prophets of the Old Testament prophesied a difficult message and ushered in the destruction of the people of God, a job nobody wanted, and yet it was necessary. When success is based upon certain worldly standards rather than obedience, we will eventually sell our souls for "success." We will look around us and define success according to some relative set of standards that is constantly changing, instead of a true definition that never changes: obedience.

In fact, nothing has revolutionized my understanding of the future more than obedience. It is absolutely freeing to know that God does not expect me to figure out the next five years or even my ultimate destination. What God calls me to is the next step of obedience. If I am simply committed to obedience then God will direct me to the places he has designed me to be.

I was recently facilitating a church planter training in San Diego, California. An older gentleman was in the room, and, after three days of intense training, he walked up to me to say thank you and to tell me his story. He lives on the Mexico/U.S. border near Tijuana and enjoys dual citizenship. He has some friends, family, and church members who live on the Mexican side and others who live on the U.S. side. He pastors one church in two locations in two different countries. Right after he finishes preaching on the Mexican side, he walks across the border, where he is picked up and driven to their Spanish-speaking location in the U.S. His church has seen numerous people come to know Jesus over the past twenty years, and now, at sixty years old, he wants to begin raising up new leaders and planting new churches. Miguel might not be the keynote speaker at any conference you attend, and he isn't someone who would naturally catch your eye, but don't tell me for a second that Miguel is not a success.

Again, if we are just seeking the external rewards and the public accolades, then at some point we will consider ourselves a failure when it's possible we are actually the definition of "success."

Let me share just one more story about one of my heroes. Her name is Reyna, and she pastors a church in Choluteca, Honduras. One day about thirty years ago, Reyna and her husband began driving into an impoverished area of the city and picking up kids to bring them to the small church they pastored. After a few months, they realized the majority of these children had not eaten anything for days, so instead of just picking them up for church, they began cooking a meal after the service. They did this for nearly eighteen years, and, as you can imagine, more and more children started coming to eat.

About twelve years ago, Reyna's husband, who was the pastor of the church, suddenly passed away from an illness. Following her husband's death, they were trying to decide what would happen to the church and who would be the next pastor. All Reyna knew was there were hungry children who were relying on them for food, so she kept cooking. After a few months, the church decided to do something radical, especially in Honduras and as a part of this particular denomination. They made her the next lead pastor of the church.

Over the past twelve years, she's continued to love the children of her city, and it has opened the door for parents, grandparents, aunts, uncles, cousins, and siblings to find Jesus. Today her small church runs a child project development center where over 210 children come each week to have their spiritual, educational, nutritional, and medical needs met. They have plans to open the only medical clinic in their area of the city where people can come and receive reduced or free medical services through the local church. The church is growing because of how many children they are reaching in their community.

Reyna wasn't just a success when she had over two hundred children in a project development center. She was a success when it was just her and her husband and three kids in the back of their pickup truck. Her story of faithfulness and obedience has increased her capacity to lead, where now her influence is over hundreds and even thousands. May we never underestimate the success of someone who continues to persevere in faithfulness.

Finishing Well

The story of Solomon teaches us the important lesson that it's not simply what we do with our lives, but it's also how we finish that ultimately determines our legacy. Was Solomon a success because he helped build the temple for God's presence, or a failure because his heart was led astray to worship other gods in the final years of his life?

I've heard it said that in your twenties and thirties your focus is usually about achieving and trying to prove yourself, while those in their forties, fifties, and sixties focus on the quality of their life and how to finish well. Wisdom doesn't always follow age, but there is no doubt that living enough life brings a perspective that many young people don't yet possess. Many people wander around forever trying to bring validity to their life by what they do, a process that many older individuals abandon after numerous failed attempts or by achieving their goals and realizing its inability to satisfy.

This might sound strange, but I've always had this weird obsession with what it means to "finish well." When I look at my story, I've realized that many of the greatest men of God I've been around in my life—pastors, family members, and spiritual giants—failed to finish well. They did many incredible things for the kingdom of God only to have a situation, an accusation, or a bad decision leave a bitter taste in the mouths of those around them.

I used to think that the struggles I faced in my twenties and thirties would lead me to the place where life would be easier and more natural in my fifties and sixties. I sort of assumed that you struggled early on but eventually learned major life lessons that made the back half of life much easier. While there might be a thread of truth to this thought, I've realized that often it's the lessons that God teaches you in your twenties and thirties that now find their application in your later years.

One area of my life where I've always been extremely intentional is learning to surround myself with older mentors who have characteristics I desire to emulate. There are three men in particular, who all happen to be pastors, who I have been considerably close to over the past several years. Two of these men serve as local pastors in the same community where I pastor, and one of them serves a community about two hours from my city. All of these men are between forty and sixty years old. It's not only the relationship I have with each of them that has taught me so much about life, but the opportunity to watch them walk through trials with such grace and steadfastness.

The reason I have learned so much from these three men is because in their lives I've seen some of the truest reflections of Jesus I've ever witnessed. Each of these men have such a genuine relationship with God, a passionate, fervent prayer life, and a ministry that flows out of this deep well of knowing Christ.

If I'm completely honest, there was still some bad theology creeping around in my soul that assumed such a genuine relationship with God would keep each of these men somewhat preserved from the "really bad stuff" in life. I mean, anyone who spent that much time in prayer and lived such a life above reproach deserved to experience the blessings of life. Instead, I've watched each of them go through immense pain and suffering over the past several years.

The first pastor and mentor has had to watch his daughter and oldest child not only run away from her faith, but dive headfirst into bad relationships, sexual promiscuity, and serious drug use. The same little girl who grew up on the pews of the church, led worship from stage, and witnessed the love and power of God on a regular basis, was now a full-blown prodigal. The second pastor and mentor is an individual who I aspire to be like in my relationship with Christ more than anyone I know. I've never been around someone who is as loving, humble and has a sensitivity to the Holy Spirit like him. And yet, I've watched him deal with physical ailment after physical ailment and was recently diagnosed with multiple sclerosis, a potentially debilitating and painful disease. I've watched as the third pastor and mentor has recently walked through the devastating impact of learning about one of his children being sexually abused by someone close to him.

You are probably fully aware that we live in a broken world. You are more than likely aware that bad things happen to really good people and all of us will experience pain and suffering. It wasn't necessarily that these men had to walk through the pain of life that impacted me, it was watching how they chose to do so. It was watching the steadfastness and resilience and even the joy in which they chose to see their circumstances.

I've realized, walking alongside them in their trials, that finishing well is not the absence of tribulations but the ability to know who you are and stay grounded in the storms of life. We are guaranteed that the storms will come (Matthew 5:45, 7:24-27) and the foundation of our lives will be shaken and tested. What we've come to read or know or experience about God will eventually require us to move into faith. And here's just the sobering reality of the palace. "The rains will come down, the streams will rise, and the winds will blow and beat against the house" (Matthew 7:25). And usually there is much more at stake in the palace than there was in the pasture: more responsibility, more people affected, and more on the line.

So maybe if we deconstruct the fairytale image of what we think life will be, and properly ground ourselves in the truth of scripture, we can live a life prepared for the battles. We can live in such a way that the unknowns and the brokenness don't knock us off course or keep us from running the race, but, instead, they just make the finish line that much sweeter.

CHAPTER 12

Valleys and Pitfalls

Three Kings

King Saul represents the naturally gifted and talented leader. 1 Samuel 9:2 tell us that not only was Saul more handsome than everyone else, but he was a head taller. Unfortunately, what comes to define the reign of Saul is not his talent or his ability, but the several moments of disobedience in which Samuel the prophet confronts him with his sin. Without much remorse or repentance, we see God reject Saul as king. From this point, it only begins to spiral further out of control as Saul is troubled by evil spirits, begins to resent David to the point of trying to kill him, and even consults a medium in 1 Samuel 28. It is a tragic story with a tragic ending, as Saul and his sons die in battle against the Philistines.

I believe Saul represents a leader who is gifted but not broken. Such leaders can display moments of incredible talent and ability, but over the long haul their lack of surrender will reveal itself. Eventually, an unbroken leader will sell out to whatever is on the throne of their heart: pride, arrogance, wealth, finances, addiction, etc. Saul is a leader who may have ascended to the palace before properly processing the pasture or the cave. What a dangerous predicament for any leader when they are thrust into a position without properly being prepared for what lies ahead of them. Eventually we find out that talent is simply not enough to sustain a leader, no matter how spectacular their gifts may be.

David has already been well-documented throughout this book. On the outside, David and Saul seem to be somewhat similar, but if you look closely you will see some startling differences. It's how they came into their positions and it's what they did in certain scenarios that reveal just how different they were. There are many examples that we could explore, but let's just look at one that I believe to be particularly revealing. Both Saul and David sinned during their time as king, and both of them were confronted by prophets, men who held them accountable before God.

In 1 Samuel 15, Samuel confronted Saul with his blatant sin of not carrying out God's commands against the Amalekites. Listen to Saul's response: "Then Saul said to Samuel, 'I have sinned. I have violated the Lord's command and your instructions. I was afraid of the men and so I give in to them. Now I beg you, forgive my sin and come back with me, so that I may worship the Lord.'" A few verses later, Saul adds this: "I have sinned. But please honor me before the elders of my people and before Israel; come back with me, so that I may worship the Lord your God" (1 Samuel 15:30).

Let's look at David's scenario. David had committed adultery with Bathsheba and then killed her husband Uriah to hide his sin—hardly the scenario that would describe "a man after the heart of God." In 2 Samuel 12, Nathan confronted David with his sin and even told him a story about a rich man who exploited a poor man to gain his only possession.

David replied by saying, "I have sinned against the Lord (period)." He followed this by putting on sackcloth and lying in ash and fasting and praying for his son. Do you see it? Can you see how it may seem like Saul and David are two very similar kings, but how the subtle differences of their repentance reveal so much of their hearts?

Saul's confession is laced with issues. He's influenced by the men he is leading, and he's quick to ask for Samuel to go back with him so that nobody will think that anything is wrong. It's important to keep up appearances as the king of Israel. It seemed as though Saul was more concerned with maintaining his reputation and looking the part than he was with the gravity of his sin. David's response, on the other hand, truly reveals the brokenness he felt about the situation. He had sinned, period. There was no softening or attempting to preserve his image in the moment. There was only mourning and repentance and crying out to God for his mercy to shine through in the moment. And that is only one example. We could discuss the way in which David would dance and worship in an "undignified" way before the Lord, or the numerous times David had a chance to kill Saul, or David seeking out members of Saul's household (Mephibosheth) in order to honor them.

And then we have Solomon. In my estimation, the story of Solomon is one of the saddest in the entire Bible. I find it somewhat bizarre that when people talk about Solomon they immediately jump to him being a man of immense wisdom or how he was responsible for building God's temple. I tend to focus on the end of his story. How did he finish his life?

Look at the end of Solomon's life:

"King Solomon, however, loved many foreign women besides Pharaoh's daughter—Moabites, Ammonites, Edomites, Sidonians and Hittites. They were from nations about which the Lord had told the Israelites, 'You must not intermarry with them, because they will surely turn your hearts after their gods.' Nevertheless, Solomon held fast to them in love. He had seven hundred wives of royal birth and three hundred concubines, and his wives led him astray. As Solomon grew old, his wives turned his heart after other gods, and his heart was not fully devoted to the Lord his God, as the heart of David his father had been. He followed Ashtoreth the goddess of the Sidonians, and Molek the detestable god of the Ammonites. So, Solomon did evil in the eyes of the Lord; he did not follow the Lord completely, as David his father had done.

On a hill east of Jerusalem, Solomon built a high place for Chemosh the detestable god of Moab, and for Molek the detestable god of the Ammonites. He did the same for all his foreign wives, who burned incense and offered sacrifices to their gods.

The Lord became angry with Solomon because his heart had turned away from the Lord, the God of Israel, who had appeared to him twice. Although he had forbidden Solomon to follow other gods, Solomon did not keep the Lord's command. So, the Lord said to Solomon, 'Since this is your attitude and you have not kept my covenant and my decrees, which I commanded you, I will most certainly tear the kingdom away from you and give it to one of your subordinates. Nevertheless, for the sake of David your father, I will not do it during your lifetime. I will tear it out of the hand of your son. Yet I will not tear the whole kingdom from him but will give him one tribe for the sake of David my servant and for the sake of Jerusalem, which I have chosen.'" (1 Kings 11:1-13)

What a horrendous end to a story and a legacy! His heart was "turned to other gods" and "not fully devoted to the Lord his God." So much so, that he began to follow and even build altars for detestable gods who were known for child sacrifice and widespread sexual promiscuity and orgies. For roughly 90 percent of Solomon's life, he was faithfully doing the work of the Lord, and yet he was a failure. After nine chapters of his incredible exploits and profound wisdom, we get thirteen verses that ultimately determined his legacy and what he left to the next generation.

What can we learn from looking at these three kings? We may love talented people or great leaders or incredible exploits, but never forget that true success and faithfulness over a lifetime will always flow from a heart fully devoted to God. For out of your heart will "flow all the issues of life" (Proverbs 4:23). David's life ended with him worn down and facing numerous challenges, including family strife, but his heart was still fully dedicated to the ways of God. Saul's life ended in a battlefield after years of frantically chasing down God's anointed leader and fighting the Philistine army. Solomon's life ended with God raising up leaders against him because of his rebellion and because he chose to worship the detestable gods of the land. Three different kings. Three different stories. All of them faced considerable hardship and made mistakes, but only one finished well.

Build an Altar

When something significant happens in your life, you stop and take in the moment. Maybe you take a picture, or maybe you take a memento to remember the occasion. I have a gray box at home full of stuff I've kept over the years. Every time I open it, all these incredible memories come flooding back. I have a rock from the ground the night I gave my heart to Jesus at youth camp. I have ticket stubs to University of Oklahoma football games and other major events throughout my life I want to remember. I have pictures, scraps of paper, and envelopes full of stuff that would mean absolutely nothing to anyone other than me.

Often throughout the Old Testament, when God would move in a miraculous way, the leaders and the people of Israel stopped and built an altar to God. This was usually accompanied by a sacrifice of some sort. This was an acknowledgement that it was God's presence, not their own effort, that brought about the miracle or the victory in battle. We need to be altar builders, constantly reminding ourselves that it is God's presence and power and provision that is our source of life and everything that is good. Because you know what happens when you don't remember? You forget. I know, pretty deep, huh?

Deuteronomy 8:2 specifically says, "Remember how the Lord your God led you all the way in the wilderness these forty years, to humble and test you in order to know what was in your heart, whether or not you would keep his commands."

Do you remember? Have you humbled yourself so that in your pride you won't think all of this was because of you? God knew that if the Israelites came out of Egypt and walked directly into the Promised Land, overpowering their enemies, they would quickly forget him. The wilderness was about God forming a people for himself. Remember, the Israelites had spent 400 years under Egyptian rule. Although they claimed to be God's people, much of their way of living was according to Egyptian tradition. In the wilderness, God tested them and gave them the law in order to form a people who would now be his own. They had lived as slaves for so long under Egyptian rule that they didn't know how to be God's chosen people, a nation walking and living in freedom.

In regard to Israel, we can read the story from beginning to end. We see God's purposes in the wilderness and how it was his desire to lead them to a place of beauty and fruitfulness. We see that the tests are in order to strengthen them and the moments of discipline are in order to redirect them back to him. Many of us have difficulty seeing God's love and grace through our tests and trials, but if we really look at the Israelites in the wilderness, then we see how every step of the journey was God trying to produce something in them, not take something from them. It was trying to bring them to a place of relationship, freedom, and trust where they could not only occupy the Promised Land but stay true to being God's covenant people. It was testing for their blessing. Even after everything God did to show his miraculous power to the Israelites, they continued to live as slaves. Even in freedom, the mindset of slavery had become their identity, and they constantly retreated back to what was comfortable.

The passage continues in Deuteronomy 8 by telling them that it is God who humbled them. He fed them with manna, he taught them to trust him, he provided them with everything they needed to live, and he disciplined them much like a father disciplines his son (Deuteronomy 8:3-5). God's discipline, which is provided to anyone who is truly loved, was preparation for where God wanted to take them. It was discipline that was leading to true life, true blessing.

"When you have eaten and are satisfied, praise the Lord your God for the good land he has given you. Be careful that you do not forget the Lord your God, failing to observe his commands, his laws and his decrees that I am giving you this day. Otherwise, when you eat and are satisfied, when you build fine houses and settle down, and when your herds and flocks grow large and your silver and gold increase and all you have is multiplied, then your heart will become proud and you will forget the Lord your God, who brought you out of Egypt, out of the land of slavery." (Deuteronomy 8:10-14)

Do you see how strategic God is about how the Israelites entered the Promised Land? Can you almost sense the concern about whether they had the character to sustain themselves in the Promised Land? God weaves this concept of remembrance all throughout the lives of the Israelites. God knew their hearts. He knew that if they got comfortable or if they just waltzed into the Promised Land, they would quickly forget it was God who delivered them. They would forget the plagues in Egypt, and how God parted the Red

Sea so they could cross on dry land, and how he miraculously provided food for them in the wilderness.

We often have spiritual amnesia, quickly forgetting all that God has done and his faithfulness throughout our lives. We are quick to forget and quick to complain when the slightest thing doesn't go our way. In the palace, we must continually build altars and present our offerings to God. We must remember that the God of the past is the God of the in-between and the God of the future. These acts are continual reminders that it is God's power, not our own, that provides the victory. They are reminders that it is not our talent or ability that is sustaining our lives, it is his hand. If we stop building altars to God, then it is only a matter of time until we start building altars unto ourselves, much like Saul.

Israel, when you are satisfied, when you finally come into the blessing, the promise that was made to you: Stay humble. Don't forget. Keep me first. Worship the Lord your God with everything you are. Build an altar to your God.

The Critics

We are human beings. We like to be liked. We naturally want to be praised, and we want to avoid rejection. It's a defense mechanism we develop from an early age in order to protect our heart and soul. Leaders, however, must learn the tricky and delicate balance of having both thick skin and a soft heart. A soft heart develops from someone who has sat at the feet of Jesus and is living a life of grace. A thick skin develops from someone who is anchored in Christ and doesn't look to derive their identity from the opinions of others.

Often the palace is accompanied by an increase in critics. As the stakes rise, so do the people who will inevitably be opposed to whatever God has called you to. It's inevitable, so you might as well come to that reality right here and now. In fact, after a while maybe you can start being encouraged by the critics, that whatever you're doing is significant enough to elicit a response from others.

Nehemiah knew that he was supposed to rebuild the walls of Jerusalem. He had the blessing of King Artaxerxes, along with access to the materials needed to rebuild the walls. Now all he needed was to get the Jews motivated around the vision of rebuilding the walls. And then we get to Nehemiah 4. There will always be a Nehemiah chapter 4 in your story, especially if it's a God-sized dream that goes far beyond your personal capacity.

"When Sanballat heard that we were rebuilding the wall, he became angry and was greatly incensed. He ridiculed the Jews." (Nehemiah 4:1)

Wait a minute, who was this Sanballat guy, and where did he come from? And why in the world did he care whether or not the Jews rebuilt their own walls? The text doesn't tell us. We can try to fill in the blanks from the context. Sanballet was an Horonite and Samaritan, and we know that both then and throughout the centuries there has always been a heavy amount of anti-Semitism from the people groups surrounding the Jews. From what we can gather, it seems as though Sanballet was ticked off because somebody was considering the well-being of the Jews. What we do know is that by Nehemiah 4:7, Sanballat the Horonite, Tobiah the Ammonite, the Arabs, the entire Ammonite people, and the people of Ashdod were conspiring against Nehemiah and the rebuilding of the wall. When the critics begin to increase, it can easily seem insurmountable.

So how do we navigate through the land of critics and opposition? First, you have to ensure that you're allowing truth and the right voices to speak to the deepest parts of your soul.

Being a pastor comes with its fair share of criticism. With over fourteen years of full-time ministry experience, there are plenty of moments when I was in the wrong and I would like to have back. There are also plenty of moments when I received unjust criticism or did something with the right heart that was taken differently than intended. As a young pastor, I gave the critics too much space in my heart. I would dwell on the words, emails, letters, and opinions that were directed my way. If you stay up late at night reading and rereading the comment section of your blog or social media posts or that one email, don't be surprised when you fall prey to the desire to please everyone. This doesn't mean that every voice you don't like or don't want to hear is the enemy or someone standing in opposition to you. It takes discernment as a leader. You must be able to distinguish between voices of destruction that stand in opposition to your calling and voices of love, correction, and even discipline—people working for your good. It's easy to start dismissing every voice in your life you don't want to hear. People often do this as a justification to do whatever they want, and it can quickly cause you to close off your heart to everyone, both negative and positive voices. But often, if we are confident enough in who we are in Christ, there are little specks of truth that can be uncovered even in unjust criticism.

I feel so incredibly blessed to pastor a healthy church full of people on mission for Jesus; honestly, I rarely have to deal with notes, comments, or emails of criticism. It's usually the "churched" people who come to our church with barrels loaded and emails already addressed that cause the biggest conflicts. Every single time our staff receives a comment, whether given in love or anger, we try to stop and ask ourselves, "Is there any truth in this or anything we need to change in order to be better stewards of the gospel?" If so, we try to own whatever we can in our response. If not, we try to honor the sender in the best possible way. You know what this does for me? It helps keep my heart soft and pliable and open to change, while simultaneously not allowing someone to hijack the mission or vision God has given us. It's a delicate balance. If I start dismissing everything I don't like, I will unintentionally harden myself to the people I need to hear.

In the palace, you must be prepared for the critics. Like David, you need to develop the heart of a warrior-poet. Able to fight off the enemies that are for your destruction and yet able to stay open to growth and change. I continually pray: God, give me a soft heart to see what you want me to see and give me thick skin to stay the course.

CHAPTER 13

Overflow

Convergence

Convergence is the understanding that God has been preparing us all along the journey. He's been forming us into the image of Christ, giving us training and experience, and helping us discover the right gift mix in our life.

Convergence is a place where our past, our experiences, and our talents and abilities come together in a place where significant kingdom impact is achieved. This term was first made popular by Robert Clinton in his book *The Making of a Leader*. In his book, Robert Clinton talks about how there may be fruitfulness in a leader's life during phases I, II, and III, but the major work is that which God is doing to and in the leader, not through him or her. During phase IV, the leader begins developing a mature fruitfulness where the individual begins to use their gift mix with considerable effectiveness. Phase V is where convergence happens. This is the place where the leader uses the best they have to offer to make a substantial impact in the lives of others.[25]

Convergence is not something we just walk right into. We don't suddenly flip on a switch and discover the place of convergence when our life has not consistently been one of service to others. Convergence begins to take shape as we are consistently giving our lives away in service to others and choosing to walk in obedience. Convergence is not a place of ease and comfort or some "perfect" place where the lessons learned in the pasture and the cave no longer apply. We don't leave those lessons behind; we now use them moving forward to help us navigate the things we will inevitably face in the palace.

When I planted a church in 2010, one of our core values was that we wanted to be a church helping people live out God's unique mission for their lives. That means everybody has a story: a past, a present, and a future. As they begin to tap into who they are in Christ and the gifts, experiences, and abilities that have shaped them, people can begin moving into God's unique missions for their lives. This is what I call "living in the sweet spot." A place where a person is operating in his or her God-given gifts, the certain graces that flow from the indwelling of the Holy Spirit in us.

As a result, we developed a growth track class we call Pathway. Over the past eight years, we have taken hundreds of people through this journey of discovery. This journey starts by taking a large poster board and developing a story timeline, from birth to present day. We ask the individual to write out all the most significant events, people, moments, and experiences (both positive and negative) on the timelines of their lives. Positive experiences go above the line, and negative experiences go below the line. We spend hours helping attendees process their stories and then lead them on a discovery of how God wants to use their experiences, abilities, and passions for his glory and purposes. We look at energizing abilities. We look at the wounds and lies that have been left because of certain people, words, or events. We look at places where they experienced God in a significant way or ways in which they seem to connect with God in a unique way.

I've walked through this process with hundreds of people and helped them process their stories. Every single time I sit down with an individual, there are significant discoveries that are made. We think we know our stories, but often we don't take the time to write it down or verbally process it with another individual. As we do this, there are themes, patterns, and "aha moments" that begin to emerge. We discover how the course of our lives has been determined by finding the right or wrong people to surround ourselves with. Or how ever since our parent's divorce when we were sixteen years old, we've believed a lie about ourselves and who God is. Or how a missions trip, summer camp, or encounter with God shaped the trajectory of our lives. Or how being hurt and betrayed by someone we loved dearly has caused us to never open our hearts to other people or to what God wants to do. There are so many God footprints in our stories if we can slow down and take the time to look. Along with these footprints, there are also arrows in our story leading us to specific things God may be directing us toward.

> *Convergence is not an overnight process. We don't move from confusion to clarity in our stories or in our ministry sweet spots in a short time. It's a process of discovery and learning to step out in faith and take small steps of obedience. It's learning to embrace the in-between: the pasture, the cave, the palace, and all the places we will visit along the way. And in the midst of this journey of faithfulness, obedience, surrender, and walking with Jesus, we are being shaped, molded, and broken in order to be given away in service to others.*

If I were to walk you through my personal life timeline, you would understand why I value certain things. Personally, one of my core values is authenticity. Growing up, both at school and church, I watched many leaders who didn't necessary live out their relationship with Christ behind closed doors. This caused doubt and confusion in my walk with Christ, and it became a stumbling block I've had to address in my spiritual walk. I've realized how much I value authentic people, because I was exposed to so many who were fake.

I also highly value one-on-one discipleship and small groups. In my story, it has been the investment of mentors in my life and small groups of three to four men that have become the catalysts for my growth in Christ. To this day, I believe the greatest level of life change happens in a small group of two to four people where you can practice confession, wrestle with questions, and learn to live out the gospel in your everyday life.

I value church planting and believe it is one of the most effective ways to reach people and make disciples. I also vividly remember what it was like to struggle and feel all alone in the church planting process as a pastor, going through intense times of difficulty and spiritual warfare. As a result, I want to give the rest of my life to helping train and resource church planters all over the world to be healthy leaders who are leading healthy churches. All these discoveries can be found in my story and have been pointing me toward living out God's unique purpose for my life.

I believe convergence is also allowing God to redeem our pain: the stories we would rather rewrite or forget. We allow God to take all the good and all the bad and all the experiences and all the abilities he has placed within us and use them to make an impact in the lives of others.

As a pastor, there is nothing I love to hear more than a redemption story. A story of something the enemy wanted to use for destruction, but God has redeemed for his purposes. Each of these stories come from people in my church who have allowed me to share their story of pain and redemption:

- Chase is an incredible young man of God and a remarkable leader. Chase has also struggled with alcohol/drug addiction over the last ten years, twice going to rehab. Chase is now healthy and continuing his road to recovery. In the meantime, he's started a small group for anybody going through recovery who wants to walk with him. He's also my oldest son's small group leader and partnered with me to help me raise my child to be passionate about Jesus. I'm incredibly grateful for Chase!

- Blaine was one of the most successful youth pastors and church planters in the country, who also had a twenty-year, life-controlling sexual addiction. After experiencing a moral failure of epic proportions and losing everything (ministry, bankruptcy, relationship with his children, marriage, etc.), Blaine has now been walking in freedom for almost seven years and launched a ministry called Chopping Wood with a vision to help one million men, including pastors, write their comeback story. He has become one of my closest friends and continues to challenge me to be a healthy man of God, husband, father, and pastor.

- Jim grew up in and out of the foster care system. His mother, who suffered from mental illness, was unable to provide any sort of consistent living situation for him, which resulted in him being in and out of homes. A family stepped into Jim's life, became his forever family, and now, as an adult, Jim is fighting on behalf of the children in our city and state who are in the welfare system. Jim's wife had an affair and left him eleven years into marriage. Jim is now remarried with three boys and is a mentor for other men who have walked through the pain of an affair or divorce. Jim is our Executive Pastor at City Church and one of my closest friends. God has used his brokenness to minister to many.

- Megan was a victim of sexual abuse growing up, and, like many, this deep wounding continued to compound throughout her life into anger. She channeled that anger into both a distrust for men and a desire to empower women. Although many of her undertakings were both genuine and worthy (anti-sex-trafficking, women's ministry, etc.), she was operating out of her hurt and pain and an area of her past that had not been fully healed. Over the past several years, I've watched her fight for her own personal freedom. Now she is operating and ministering out of a passion for empowering women that flows from a freedom she has found in Christ, not an anger for what happened to her.

Jesus does not take good people and make them better. He takes broken, crushed people and he resurrects them, making them new. I believe nothing disarms the power of the enemy like someone who takes the pain, brokenness, and darkness of the cave and chooses to see God's beauty, his grace, and his goodness in all of it. That is redemption. That is not only allowing God to put the pieces back together, but then allowing God to use it to draw others to him. Why is Easter Sunday such a time of joy and celebration? Because we know the darkness and despair of living in the reality of Friday and Saturday.

I believe that often in our palace experiences God takes the lessons of the pasture or the pain of the cave and uses them to make a significant impact in the life of another person: Discipling a young man. Walking with our children through a season of spiritual confusion. Sitting with a friend who has just lost her father. God never wastes our story. We often believe our lives should be a photo of a field full of wildflowers, with innumerable blessings as far as the eye can see. Instead, what often happens is that our lives become a photo of a single flower growing between the crack in the concrete. The field of wildflowers will come one day when Christ returns. In the meantime, we will gladly accept a God who makes all things new.

Ishmaels and Isaacs

There is a joy and beauty of operating in the palace that is hard to describe. It's the sweet spot that God designed us to experience. This is the place where our identities in Christ and the unique abilities God has given us merge together and overflow in love and compassion and service to others. We know when we're operating in this place, because even though there are difficulties and days that are draining, we know that God has positioned us for this purpose.

I've known from such a young age that God had called me to the teach the Bible. I remember sitting in my seat at church as young as twelve or thirteen years old, trying to write down every word my pastor said. I would go back home and read over the passage and begin studying on my own. I love being able to illuminate the scriptures for someone in a way where the Bible became alive and real. As of today, our church currently has three services every Sunday morning. I'm not going to say that at times it's not tiresome, but I love teaching so much that, even though I leave the church every Sunday at 1:30 p.m. mentally and physically exhausted, inside I am bursting with joy. Every week I get the opportunity to illuminate God's word and share the power of the gospel with someone. It truly is incredible to get the opportunity to operate within your passion and calling.

Finding this sweet spot, however, is a process of discovery that almost never ends. There is an unfortunate and dangerous tendency to assume you are both deserving and entitled to operate in a place of convergence right away or whenever you want. It's recent college grads who are turning down good jobs because it doesn't fall within their sweet spot of ability and passion. It's young adults who are experiencing incredible levels of discontentment because they are thirty years old and not making a six-figure salary. It's a middle-aged man who always assumed he would be farther along by age forty-five. It's the elderly couple who are facing the difficulties of the workplace after not practicing good stewardship in their younger years.

Let's be very clear! This place of convergence doesn't happen quickly or overnight, and it's not something you get the luxury of just walking into. Convergence is choosing the long way. It's the realization that experiencing convergence in your life is a byproduct of hard work and effort and perseverance and faithfulness. It's choosing the road less traveled, or doing the menial job with excellence, or faithfully serving in an area that you aren't particularly passionate about. Sometimes it even means navigating the transitions of life and finding ourselves back in a place of obscurity after experiencing the mountaintop of influence or leadership.

I love how Todd Henry describes the process in his book *Die Empty*. "Too many people want to come out of the gate with a clear understanding of their life's mission. There is no one thing that you are wired to do, and there are many ways you can add value to the world, while operating in your sweet spot. However, these opportunities will only become clear over time as you act. They will develop slowly like film in a darkroom, giving you clues as you experiment, fail, and succeed. You have to try different things, and devote yourself to developing your skills and intuition, before you will begin to see noticeable patterns and unique value. Patience is required. This is a long-arc game, but it must begin now."[26]

There is a huge difference between trying to make something happen out of our own efforts and walking into the calling of God. Convergence is something we walk into over time, as we are submitting our lives and abilities to God. It's not immediate or produced through our efforts. It can be extremely difficult, however, for many people to navigate this tension. How do I know if God is asking me to take a big leap of faith or if he's asking me to remain faithful?

In the Old Testament, there was a profound difference between Isaac and Ishmael. One was a child of promise, an integral part of God's plan of redemption for the people of Israel and the entire world. The other was birthed out of a lack of faith, a desire to produce something outside of God's direction and timing. One would bring incredible blessing to a nation; the other would remain a thorn in their side for generations. Stepping out into God's call for our life can be one of the greatest, life-changing, risk-filled adventures imaginable. When we operate in our own timing, however, it can also be full of pain, remorse, and even cause us to question the goodness of God.

Much like Abraham, God doesn't necessarily give up on us when we have our Ishmael moments. We may be forced to live with some of the consequences of those decisions, but thankfully when you're learning to live a life of faith, trust, and surrender to God's will, there is grace. There is space to get it wrong and still be loved, accepted, and called – this is grace. In Abraham's scenario, the birth of Ishmael did not eliminate the birth of Isaac, but it did cause division; something Israel would battle for years to come.

I've spent the last fourteen years of my life working closely with college students and young adults. I've seen my fair share of Abrahams. Young, ambitious individuals who get an idea, have an issue they want to see addressed, want a change of scenery, or simply feel the pressure go and succeed. These Ishmaels are usually surrounded by all the correct spiritual jargon with maybe even a declaration of "hearing from God." And I believe they often do hear from God. I also believe that hearing his voice can be difficult, especially when someone is not attuned to what the Holy Spirit is saying. I've also learned that Ishmaels are usually lacking one or many of the following things that are necessary when determining God's will for our lives.

First, I believe God often uses levels of spiritual authority. God moves and speaks through channels of authority in our lives as we are submitting ourselves under their covering. So we must ask ourselves these questions: Who are we submitted to, and how have we sought their direction, wisdom, and counsel in this decision? How important was spiritual authority in the life of David in 2 Samuel 12?

Second, God often speaks to us through scripture. Does it align with the Word of God? Does this decision align with the truth of scripture and the character and nature of God revealed through his Word? God is continually speaking through scripture, which is living and active and continually able to lead us towards the truth of who God is.

Third, I believe we must test the motives and condition of our heart. Where is my heart and what are my motives? Am I running from something or chasing something, or am I in a position of surrender? It is far too easy to misquote a scripture or assume something about God that is not derived from the truth of who God is but from our own ulterior motives.

Fourth would be the power of prayer and fasting. Have you sought God and positioned yourself to hear? Prayer gets us out of our flesh and into a position to truly hear and receive. Fasting breaks down some of the fleshly barriers that can stand in our way of hearing what God is saying.

Even if you're moving out into your Isaac moment, it doesn't mean it will be easy. It doesn't mean it won't require radical faith and risk, it simply means that you've spent enough time in the pasture that your heart and faith has been tested and you're ready to do battle with the Goliath standing in front of you. In the waiting, you will be tempted to produce an Ishmael, helping God fulfill his promise by taking the matter into your own hands. Ishmael is what we produce when we are tired of waiting and choose to take over. Don't be misled. Remain faithful to God and watch as he produces the Isaac you've been waiting on.

In 2008, I was almost three years into a college/young adult pastoral position that I loved. I was twenty-four years old, newly married, and finishing up my graduate degree in theological studies. I had felt this pull toward church planting ever since I had joined a church planting team back in 2002. It was always in the back of my mind, but it was also something I had honestly shelved for a future date—a time when I was more mature, more prepared, and when I didn't look like I was seventeen years old. I had a group of friends in ministry who had been dreaming about planting a church. I remember going on an eight-hour road trip with one of them as he was trying to talk me into joining their team and moving my family to a new city. The whole concept was laughable to me at the moment. Why would I leave the amazing opportunity I had right then for a risky adventure that may or may not pan out?

It's hard to describe what I experienced in the next two to three months, but I knew God was doing something in me. I've never had trouble sleeping, and I'm not the kind of guy that receives dreams from God in my sleep. But night after night I laid awake in my bed staring at the ceiling, wondering if God was truly calling me to this new work or if I was just restless and confused. In the days that followed, I told my wife about what I felt God was doing. We began making it a matter of prayer and fasting. One day I remember writing down in my journal what God had been speaking to me about radical faith and trusting God with no safety net and no Plan B.

Through this time of prayer and fasting, I knew God was calling us out of the safety of the known and into the unknown. We had been faithful where God had placed us, and we had honored the authorities in our lives, and now God was calling us into this new territory. Let me be honest about what happened next. In my mind, I knew it wouldn't be easy, but I also had developed an understanding that when you are obedient to God's call, there are significantly fewer obstacles to navigate.

From the moment we packed up the U-Haul truck and moved to our city, the next sixteen months would become the most challenging I had ever experienced. It seemed like every single week we were experiencing these amazing miracles from God, along with horrendous disasters we never signed up for. The spiritual warfare during this time was the most intense I had ever faced. In the first eight months of our church plant, I lost my best friend, and I watched one of my other closest friends (and a fellow staff member) go through the devastation of an affair and divorce. During this sixteen-month journey, I sought God like never before, asking for directions and answers to dilemmas we were facing and the staff of people I was now responsible for leading. I must admit that I never received clarity or specifics during this difficult time, but I could sense that God was doing something transformative deep within my soul. The only "word" I remember God speaking to my soul over and over again was simply this: persevere.

I didn't receive any sort of special revelation or new growth formula or some powerful spiritual "breakthrough." The only thing I received was a confirmation that God was still in control in the middle of the mess. That all the struggle didn't mean that God was absent or had abandoned this cause. Sometimes the formula for faith is as simple as holding on.

Even in the struggle, God had directed us in his timing, and we had responded in obedience. This endeavor was not an Ishmael-moment when we had tried to birth something in our own effort or lack of patience. I knew that this step of faith was an Isaac-moment, a response of faith and obedience that God had called us to walk out. God, give us the courage to step off the ledge of faith in our Isaac-moments, and give us the wisdom to wait patiently in order to avoid our Ismael-moments.

CHAPTER 14

Legacy

Living in the Right Now

Most people in their twenties and thirties spend very little time thinking about their legacy. They may spend a few moments thinking about legacy during a sermon or a funeral or an inspirational talk, reflecting on what they want to leave behind. Then, inevitably, they jump back into the normal rhythms and routines of life, and those thoughts are relegated to the "good intentions" category of life. With age, however, often comes an increased fascination concerning what you will leave behind, how you will be remembered, and what impact you have made.

When our four kids were babies, I used to occasionally take the middle-of-the-night feeding. Let me just go on record and publicly say that for every one shift I took, my wife took twenty shifts. She's my hero! I always had a handful of songs I would sing to my kids while rocking them, and each of them started to memorize the words to these songs as they got older. One of the songs was "10,000 Reasons" by Matt Redman (or as my kids always called it "Bless the Lord, Oh My Soul). I honestly believe this song to be a modern-day hymn that people generations from now will be singing, much like we do for many of the classics today.

I must admit that over the years I've become somewhat obsessed with the words to this song, especially the third verse. *And on that day when my strength is failing. The end draws near and my time has come. Still my soul will sing Your praise unending. 10,000 years and then forever more.*[27]

The words seem rather simple, and yet as I grow older I realize how easily we can be led astray throughout our lives. There are plenty of opportunities to become bitter and cynical, and a number of idols can lead our hearts astray, much like Solomon.

I've also learned that legacy has less to do with my resume or accomplishments and more to do with the condition of my heart and my relationship with my heavenly Father. In fact, with each year I get older, my understanding of legacy starts to shift a little bit. Just a few years ago, my legacy was always connected to how many people I reached or how healthy my church was or how many church planters we trained and released. And now I realize that my greatest legacy will be the condition of my heart and my relationship with Christ. When my time has come, will I be filled with regret, frantically moving about trying to get things in order, or will I truly be able to "sing your praise unending"? Will my heart sing out from the deepest parts of me, "Bless the Lord, oh my soul"?

Recently, one of my personal heroes, Eugene Peterson, passed away and is now experiencing his eternal joy. As a young man, Eugene Peterson deeply influenced my understanding and role of what a pastor is. It was said that as his close friends and family gathered around him during his final moments, he looked at them and uttered the words, "Let's go!" That may seem rather simple and non-newsworthy to you, but, let me tell you, those are not words you utter at the end of your life unless you've truly discovered something. Only through a deep, abiding relationship with Christ and a complete and utter confidence in the goodness of God do we look at the end of our life and realize it is only the beginning! You don't utter those words out of fear or uncertainty, but by a faith that has been tested, tried, and found true.

Years ago, one of my mentors led me through a spiritual growth practice of writing a legacy letter. I was thirty years old at the time, and I was to write a letter to my sixty-five-year-old self. I sat down for several hours writing a letter to myself, my wife, and each of my children. What was most revealing about the letter? As I wrote, I wasn't necessarily writing about any of my accomplishments. In fact, I spent two whole pages just reminding myself that all the achievements in life wouldn't make me a success. Here's just a small sample of the letter:

Let me remind you that your desire to achieve and accomplish will never satisfy the deepest longings of your soul. There's not enough ministry wins, awards, verbal praises, or impacted lives that will quench that thirst. Lord knows you've tried. One thing old age can bring you is clarity. Hindsight has a way of bringing things into focus. There is something about age that begins to strip you of all your glory, accolades and good intentions and reveals your true identity. Did you fall deeply in love with God, or did you fall in love with the idea of falling in love with God? Did you secretly try to achieve your way into his arms or did you learn to really rest; fully trusting in his complete and total goodness? Did you foster and develop a genuine relationship with your heavenly Father, or did you just know about him? Can I tell that how you answer these questions may just be the "secret" to unlocking joy, peace, love, and "success."

The rest of the letter was about loving well. Loving God. Loving people. Living out of this deep, abiding relationship with Christ. Living out of the overflow. It was reminding my children that God was good and that he could be trusted through every moment of life. That their greatest accomplishment in life could not be quantified or measured, because it can only be found in him.

The message of this book did not start out as a book. It started as a process that God was trying to reveal to me. In fact, years ago when I first started thinking about writing this down and turning it into a book, I thought the last section, "The Palace," would look very different. I thought it would be full of advice and tips about how to move out into your ministry sweet spot. Over the past several years, my understand of "arriving" or the "palace" has been drastically transformed along the way. I had always assumed that the palace was a place, a physical reality. I've since learned that it is more of a spiritual reality that ends up determining our physical realities. The process is not a stepping stone to get somewhere else or to achieve what I want; but he is my destination and everything I've inwardly been searching for. It is this single reality that has taught me to stop striving and trying to manufacture my future. It is this reality that has allowed me to sit in the moment in peace and quiet confidence: knowing who I am and knowing that my God is fully in control of the future. It is this reality that has caused me to stop chasing, frantically moving about searching for some elusive "thing."

It's possible that as you're reading this book you find yourself in the pasture. If so, I challenge you to not only embrace this season, but to fall in love with it. Don't get distracted or antsy or begin thinking that life only begins when you _____. True identity, which leads to true joy, is often discovered on the backside of the place we didn't necessarily want to be. David walked out of the pasture with a confidence in God and an assurance of who he was: the very things that would become foundational as he entered the cave.

Maybe today you're in the middle of the cave. Just like David, this wasn't in your five-year-plan, and the cave feels like the end of a dream or a painful reality that will never end. You may be tested to let go of the dream or to allow your difficult situation to become a barometer for God's heart towards you, but please don't give in to the lie. On the other side of the cave can be a depth and revelation of God's faithfulness that is found no other way than by walking with God through the brokenness of life. The pain, the scars, and the brokenness not only speak to his grace in our lives, but they also fix our hearts on our future hope and kingdom to come. Only through this process of surrender will our hearts be fully his.

Or maybe today you're experiencing the palace. Maybe you're experiencing the joy of living out of the overflow and the place of convergence. Don't forget what brought you to this place and what will sustain you in this place. Maybe the palace is not quite as idyllic as you had imagined it would be. Remember, the palace is not a place where we leave the realities of the pasture or cave behind, but where we continue to live in them and allow them to fuel our purpose and calling.

More than anything, my prayer for you is that you STOP CHASING, you learn to TRUST in God's complete goodness for you, and you find PEACE in Christ. You don't have to search. You don't have to have it all figured out.

You don't have to live in fear or worry about missing God's will. My prayer is that you embrace the waiting and the in-between as the very place where you meet God, find life, and experience real transformation. That you let go of every false idol, unmet expectation, season of difficulty, and broken dream, and you realize that everything you've ever wanted, desired, or been searching for is found right now in him.

Notes

[1] James Bryan Smith, *The Good and Beautiful God* (InterVarsity Press: Downers Grove, 2009).

[2] Michael Harter, eds., *Hearts on Fire: Praying with Jesuits* (Loyola Press: Washington D.C., 2005).

[3] Dallas Willard, *The Divine Conspiracy* (HarperCollins: New York, 1998).

[4] John C. Maxwell, *Failing Forward* (Thomas Nelson: Nashville, 2000).

[5] John Maxwell, ARC Conference, 2014.

[6] Robert Clinton, *The Making of a Leader* (NavPress: Colorado Springs, 1988).

[7] Henri Nouwen, *The Return of the Prodigal Son* (Doubleday: New York, 1992).

[8] Ann Voskamp, blog: https://annvoskamp.com.

[9] Tim Elmore, *The Secret to Raising Emotionally Healthy Kids*, https://growingleaders.com/blog/the-secret-to-raising-emotionally-healthy-kids/

[10] Henri Nouwen, *Finding My Way Home* (The Crossroad Publishing Company: New York, 2001).

[11] Paul Miller, *A Praying Life* (NavPress: Colorado Springs, 2009).

[12] Eugene Peterson, *Earth and Altar,* (InterVarsity Press; Illinois, 1985).

[13] Scott Anthony, "The Planning Fallacy and the Innovator's Dilemma," August 1, 2012, https://hbr.org/2012/08/the-planning-fallacy-and-the-i

[14] Paul Miller, *A Praying Life* (NavPress: Colorado Springs, 2009).

[15] C. S. Lewis, *The Screwtape Letters* (HarperCollins: New York, 1942).

[16] Macrina Diederkehr, *Seasons of the Heart* (HarperCollins: New York, 1991).

[17] www.christianpost.com/news/youversion-bible-app-reveals-most-read-bible-verse-2017-209505/

[18] Brennan Manning, *Ruthless Trust* (HarperCollins: New York, 2000).

[19] Thomas Merton, *Thoughts in Solitude* (Farrar, Straus & Giroux: New York, 1958**).**

[20] Morton Kelley, *The Other Side of Silence* (Paulist Press: New Jersey, 1976).

[21] Brene Brown: "The Power of Vulnerability," June 1, 2010, www.ted.com/talks/brene_brown_on_vulnerability

[22] Wayne Muller, *Sabbath* (New York: Bantam Books, 1999).

[23] Tom Ashbrook, *Mansions of the Heart* (Jossey-Bass: San Francisco, 2009).

[24] Andy Stanley, *Visioneering* (Multnomah: Colorado Springs, 1999).

[25] Robert Clinton, *The Making of a Leader* (NavPress: Colorado Springs, 1988).

[26] Todd Henry, *Die Empty* (Penguin Group: New York, 2015).

[27] Matt Redman, Song: "10,000 Reasons."

ABOUT THE AUTHOR

Matt and his wife Lindsay live in Tulsa, OK with their four children and serve as Lead Pastors of City Church, a thriving church committed to disciple-making, sending, and church multiplication. Matt also serves as the Executive Director of Seed Network, a church planting organization committed to creating a safe place for radical church multiplication.

For additional information:
- http://www.mattnelsononline.com
- https://citychurchtulsa.com
- http://seed.network

179

Printed in Poland
by Amazon Fulfillment
Poland Sp. z o.o., Wrocław